INTELLIGENCE

INTELLIGENCE

The Creative Response
to Now

OSHO

·

Insights for a
New Way of Living

St. Martin's Griffin ✹ New York

www.stmartins.com

www.osho.com.

All books in the Insights for a New Way of Living series are created from
selected excerpts from the archive of original works by the author.

OSHO is a registered trademark of Osho International Foundation,
used with permission.

Library of Congress Cataloging-in-Publication Data

Osho, 1931–1990.
Intelligence: the creative response to now / Osho.—1st St. Martin's Griffin ed.
    p.   cm. — (Insights for a new way of living)
    ISBN 0-312-32072-8
    EAN 978-0312-32072-0
    1. Intellect. I. Title. II. Series: Osho, 1931–1990. Insights for a new way of living.
    BP605.R34053 2004
    299'.93—dc22   2003026318

10   9   8   7   6   5

Contents

Contents

Foreword

INTELLIGENCE IS NOT WHAT YOU THINK

First, know well that intellectuality is not intelligence. To be intellectual is to be phony; it is pretending intelligence. It is not real because it is not yours, it is borrowed.

Intelligence is the growth of inner consciousness. It has nothing to do with knowledge, it has something to do with meditativeness. An intelligent person does not function out of his past experience; he functions in the present. He does not react, he responds. Hence he is always unpredictable; one can never be certain what he is going to do.

A Catholic, a Protestant, and a Jew were talking to a friend who said he had just been given six months to live.

"What would you do," the man asked the Catholic, "if your doctor gave you six months to live?"

"Ah!" said the Catholic. "I would give all my belongings to the church, take communion every Sunday, and say my Hail Marys regularly."

"And you?" he asked the Protestant.

"I would sell everything and go on a world cruise and have a great time!"

"And you?" he said to the Jew.
"Me? I would see another doctor."

That is intelligence!

INTELLIGENCE

INTELLIGENCE—
A GIFT OF NATURE

I ntelligence is intrinsic to life. Intelligence is a natural quality of life. Just as fire is hot and air is invisible and water flows downward, so is life intelligent.

Intelligence is not an achievement. You are *born* intelligent. Trees are intelligent in their own way, they have enough intelligence for their own life. Birds are intelligent, so are animals. In fact, what religions mean by God is only this—that the universe is intelligent, that there is intelligence hidden everywhere. And if you have eyes to see, you can see it everywhere. Life is intelligence.

Only man has become unintelligent. Man has damaged the natural flow of life. Except in man, there is no unintelligence. Have you ever seen a bird you can call stupid? Have you ever seen an animal you can call idiotic? No, such things happen only to man. Something has gone wrong.

> Have you ever seen a bird you can call stupid? Have you ever seen an animal you can call idiotic? No, such things happen only to man. Something has gone wrong.

Man's intelligence has been damaged, corrupted, has been crippled.

And meditation is nothing but the undoing of that damage. Meditation will not be needed at all if man is left alone. If the priest and the politician do not interfere with man's intelligence, there will be no need for any meditation. Meditation is medicinal—first you have to create the disease, then meditation is needed. If the disease is not there, meditation is not needed. And it is not accidental that the words *medicine* and *meditation* come from the same root. It is medicinal.

Each child is born intelligent, and the moment the child is born, we pounce upon him and start destroying his intelligence, because intelligence is dangerous to the political structure, to the social structure, to the religious structure. It is dangerous to the pope, it is dangerous to the priest, it is dangerous to the leader. It is dangerous to the status quo, the establishment. Intelligence is naturally rebellious. Intelligence cannot be forced into any servitude. Intelligence is very assertive, individual. Intelligence cannot be forced into a mechanical imitation.

People have to be converted to carbon copies; their originality has to be destroyed, otherwise all the nonsense that has existed on the earth would be impossible. You need a leader because first you have been made unintelligent—otherwise there would be no need for any leader. Why should you follow anybody? You will follow your intelligence. If somebody wants to become a leader, then one thing has to be done: Your intelligence has to be destroyed somehow. You have to be shaken from your very roots, you have to be made afraid. You have to be made unconfident in yourself—that is a must. Only then can the leader come in.

If you are intelligent, you will solve your problems yourself. Intelligence is enough to solve all the problems. In fact, whatsoever problems are created in life, you have more intelligence than those problems. It is a provision, it is a gift of nature. But there are ambitious people who want to rule, dominate; there are ambitious madmen—they create fear in you. Fear is like rust: It destroys all intelligence. If you want to destroy somebody's intelligence, the first thing needed is to create fear: Create hell and make people afraid. When people are afraid of hell, they will go and bow down to the priest. They will listen to the priest. If they don't listen to the priest then they will face hellfire—naturally they are afraid. They have to protect themselves from hellfire, and the priest is needed. The priest becomes a must.

I have heard about two men who were partners in a business. Their business was very unique and they used to travel around the country. One partner would go into a town, and in the night he would go around and throw coal tar on people's windows, and then disappear by morning. After two or three days, the other would come. He would offer to clean the coal tar from people's windows. And people would pay, of course—they had to pay. They were partners in the same business. One would do the damage, the other would come to undo it.

> ﹏
> If you want to destroy somebody's intelligence, the first thing needed is to create fear: create hell and make people afraid.

Fear has to be created, and greed has to be created. Intelligence is not greedy. You will be surprised to know that an intelligent man is never greedy. Greed is part of unintelligence. You hoard for tomorrow because you are not confident that tomorrow you will be able to tackle your life, otherwise why hoard? You become misers, you become greedy, because you don't know whether tomorrow your intelligence will be capable of coping with life or not. Who knows? You are not confident about your intelligence so you hoard, you become greedy. An intelligent person is not afraid, is not greedy.

Greed and fear go together—that's why heaven and hell go together. Hell is fear, heaven is greed. Create fear in people and create greed in people—make them as greedy as possible. Make them so greedy that life cannot satisfy them, then they will go to the priest and to the leader. Then they will start fantasizing about some future life where their foolish desires and stupid fantasies will be fulfilled. Watch it—to demand the impossible is to be unintelligent.

An intelligent person is perfectly satisfied with the possible. He works for the probable; he never works for the impossible and the improbable, no. He looks at life and its limitations. He is not a perfectionist. A perfectionist is neurotic. If you are a perfectionist you will become neurotic.

For example, if you love a woman and you ask absolute fidelity, you will go mad and she will go mad. This is not possible. Absolute fidelity means she will not even think, she will not even dream of another man— this is not possible. Who are you? Why has she fallen in love with you? Because you are a man. If she can fall in love with you, why can't she think of others? That possibility remains open. And how is she going to manage if she sees some beautiful person walking by and a desire arises in her? Even to say "This man is beautiful" is to desire—the desire has entered. You only say that something is beautiful when you feel it is worthy of being possessed, of being enjoyed. You are not indifferent.

Now if you ask absolute fidelity—as people have asked—then there is bound to be conflict, and you will remain suspicious. And you will remain suspicious because you know your mind, too—you think of other women, so how can you trust that your woman is not thinking of other men? You know what you are thinking, so you know she is thinking the same things. Now distrust arises, conflict, agony. The love that was possible has become impossible because of an impossible desire.

People ask that which cannot be done. You want security for the future, which is not possible. You want absolute security for tomorrow—it cannot be guaranteed; it is not in the nature of life. An intelligent person knows that it is not in the nature of life. The future remains open—the bank can go bankrupt, the wife can escape with somebody else, the husband can die, the children may prove unworthy. Who knows about tomorrow? You may fall ill, you may become crippled. Who knows about tomorrow?

To ask security for tomorrow means to remain in constant fear. Security is not possible, so when you are afraid of insecurity, your fear cannot be destroyed. Fear will be there, you will be trembling—and

meanwhile the present moment is being missed. With the desire for security in the future you are destroying the present, which is the only life
available. And more and more will you become shaken, afraid, greedy.

A child is born; a child is a very, very open phenomenon, utterly intelligent. But we jump upon him, we start destroying his intelligence. We
start creating fear in him. You call it teaching, you call it making the child
capable of coping with life. He is unafraid, and you create fear in him.

And your schools, colleges, universities—they all make him more
and more unintelligent. They demand foolish things. They demand foolish things to be memorized, things in which the child and his natural intelligence cannot see any point. For what? That child cannot see the
point. Why cram these things into his head? But the university says, the
college says, the home, the family, the well-wishers say, "Cram! You don't
know now, but later on you will know why it is needed."

Cram history, all the nonsense that people have been doing to other
people, all the madness—study it! And the child cannot see the point.
What does it matter when a certain king ruled England, from what date
to what date? But he has to memorize those stupid things. Naturally, his
intelligence becomes more and more burdened, crippled. More and more
dust collects on his intelligence. By the time a person comes back from
the university, he is unintelligent—the university has done its job. It is
very rare that someone can graduate from the university and still remain
intelligent. Very few people have been able to escape the university, to
avoid it, pass through the university and yet save their intelligence—very
rarely. It is such a great mechanism to destroy you.

The moment you become educated, you have become unintelligent.
Can't you see this? The educated person behaves very unintelligently. Go to the primitive people who have never been educated, and
you will find a pure intelligence functioning.

I have heard . . .

A woman was trying to open a tin, and she could not figure
out how to do it. So she went to look in the cookbook. By the

time she looked into the book, the cook had opened it. She came back, and she was surprised. She asked the cook, "How did you do it?"

He said, "Lady, when you don't know how to read, you have to use your intelligence!"

Yes, it is right. When you don't know how to read you have to use your intelligence. What else can you do? The moment you start reading—those three dangerous Rs, when you have become capable in them—you need not be intelligent, the books will take care of it.

Have you watched it? When a person starts typing, his handwriting is lost; then his handwriting is no longer beautiful. There is no need: The typewriter takes care of it. If you carry a calculator in your pocket, you will forget all mathematics—there is no need. Sooner or later everybody will be carrying small computers. They will have all the information of an *Encyclopaedia Britannica,* and then there will be no need for you to be intelligent at all; the computer will take care of it.

Go to the primitive people, the uneducated people, the villagers, and you will find a subtle intelligence. Yes, they are not very informed, that is true. They are not knowledgeable, that is true—but they are tremendously intelligent. Their intelligence is like a flame with no smoke around it.

The society has done something wrong with the human being—for certain reasons. It wants you to be slaves, it wants you to be always afraid. It wants you to be always greedy, it wants you to be always ambitious, it wants you to be always competitive. It wants you to be unloving, it wants you to be full of anger and hatred. It wants you to remain weak, imitative—carbon copies. It does not want you to become original and unique and rebellious, no. That's why your intelligence has been destroyed.

Meditation is needed only to undo what the society has done. Meditation is negative: It simply negates the damage, it destroys the illness. And once the illness has gone, your well-being asserts itself of its own accord.

In the last century it has gone too far: Universal education has been a calamity. And remember, I am not against education, I am against *this* education. There is a possibility of a different kind of education which will be helpful in sharpening your intelligence, not destroying it; which will not burden it with unnecessary facts, which will not burden it with unnecessary knowledge, which will not burden it at all, but rather will help it to become more radiant, fresh, young.

This education only makes you capable of memorizing. That education will make you capable of more clarity. This education destroys your inventiveness. That education will help you to become more inventive.

For example, the education that I would like in the world will not require a child to answer in the old stereotyped way. It will not encourage repetition, parroting. It will encourage inventiveness. Even if the invented answer is not as right as the copied answer can be, still it will appreciate the child who has brought a new answer to an old problem. Certainly the child's answer cannot be as right as Socrates' answer—naturally, a small child's answer cannot be as exact as that of Albert Einstein. But to ask that the child's answer should be as right as that of Albert Einstein is foolish. If the child is inventive, he or she is moving in the right direction; one day the child will become an Albert Einstein. If he is trying to create something new naturally, he has his limitations, but just his effort in trying to create something new should be appreciated, should be praised.

Education should not be competitive. People should not be judged against each other. Competitiveness is very violent and very destructive.

> Meditation is needed only to undo what the society has done. Meditation is negative: it simply negates the damage, it destroys the illness. And once the illness has gone, your well-being asserts itself of its own accord.

Somebody is not good at mathematics and you call him mediocre. And he may be good at carpentry, but nobody looks at that. Somebody is not good at literature and you call her stupid—and she will be good at music, at dance.

A real education will help people to find *their* life where they can be fully alive. If a child is born to be a carpenter, then that is the right thing for him to do. There should be nobody to enforce anything else. This world can become such a great, intelligent world if a child is allowed to be himself or herself, helped, supported in every way, and nobody interferes. In fact, nobody manipulates the child. If the child wants to become a dancer, then that is good—dancers are needed. Much dance is needed in the world. If the child wants to become a poet, good. Much poetry is needed; there is never enough. If the child wants to become a carpenter or a fisherman, perfectly good. If the child wants to become a woodcutter—perfectly good. There is no need to become a president or a prime minister. In fact, fewer people will become interested in those targets; it will be a blessing.

Right now everything is topsy-turvy. One who wanted to become a carpenter has become a doctor; one who wanted to become a doctor has become a carpenter. Everybody is in somebody else's place, hence so much unintelligence—everybody is doing somebody else's job. Once you start seeing it, you will understand why people are behaving unintelligently.

In India we have been meditating deeply, and we have found one word: *Swadharma,* self-nature. That carries the greatest implication for a future world. Krishna has said, *Swadharme nadhanam shreyah;* "It is good to die in your own self-nature, following your self-nature." *Per dharmo bavaha baha;* "Somebody else's nature is very dangerous." Don't become an imitator. Just be yourself.

I have heard . . .

Bill always wanted to go moose hunting so he saved up enough money and went to the north woods. There he was fitted out with necessary equipment and the storekeeper advised him to hire Pierre, the greatest moose caller in the land.

"It's true," said the storekeeper, "that Pierre is expensive, but he has a sexy quality in his call that no moose can resist."

"How does that work?" asked Bill.

"Well," said the other, "Pierre will spot a moose at three hundred yards, then cup his hands and make his first call. When the moose hears that, he will become excited with anticipatory desire and approach to two hundred yards. Pierre will then call again, putting a bit more oomph into it, and the moose will skip with eager glee to a distance of a hundred yards. This time Pierre really gives his call a sexy delivery, prolonging it a bit, which impels the moose, agitated with carnal intent, to come to a point only twenty-five yards away from you. And that is the time, my friend, for you to aim and shoot."

"Suppose I miss?" wondered Bill.

"Oh, that would be terrible!" said the other.

"But why?" asked Bill.

"Because then poor Pierre gets mated."

That has happened to man—imitating, imitating. Man has completely lost the vision of his own reality. The Zen people say: Seek out your original face. Find out what is your authenticity. Who are you? If you don't know who you are, you will always be in some accident—always. Your life will be a long series of accidents, and whatever happens it will never be satisfying. Discontent will be the only taste of your life.

You can see it around you. Why do so many people look so dull, bored, just passing the days somehow? Passing tremendously valuable time which they will not be able to recover—and passing with such dullness, as if only waiting for death. What has happened to so many people? Why don't they have the same freshness as the trees? Why doesn't man have the same song as the birds? What has happened to human beings? One thing has happened: Man has been imitating. Man has been trying to become somebody else. Nobody is at home. Everybody is knocking at somebody else's door; hence discontent, dullness, boredom, anguish.

An intelligent person will try just to be himself, whatsoever the cost. An intelligent person will never copy, will never imitate. He will never parrot. An intelligent person will listen to his own intrinsic call. He will feel his own being and move accordingly, whatsoever the risk.

There is risk! When you copy others there is less risk. When you don't copy anybody you are alone—there is risk! But life happens only to those who live dangerously. Life happens only to those who are adventurous, who are courageous, almost daredevils—only to them does life happen. Life does not happen to lukewarm people.

Intelligence is trust in your own being. Intelligence is adventure, thrill, joy. Intelligence is to live in this moment, not to hanker for the future. Intelligence is not to think of the past and not to bother about the future—the past is no more, the future is not yet. Intelligence is to make the utmost use of the present moment that is available. The future will come out of it. If this moment has been lived in delight and joy, the next moment is going to be born out of it. It will bring more joy naturally, but there is no need to bother about it. If my today has been golden, my tomorrow will be even more golden. From where will it come? It will grow out of today.

If this life has been a benediction, my next life will be a higher benediction. From where can it come? It will grow out of me, out of my *lived* experience. So an intelligent person is not concerned about heaven and hell, is not concerned about the afterlife, is not concerned even about God, is not concerned

> Intelligence is not to think of the past and not to bother about the future—the past is no more, the future is not yet. Intelligence is to make the utmost use of the present moment that is available.

even about the soul. An intelligent person simply lives intelligently, and God and the soul and heaven and nirvana all follow naturally.

You live in belief; belief is unintelligent. Live through knowing; knowing is intelligence. And intelligence is meditation.

Unintelligent people also meditate, but certainly they meditate in an unintelligent way. They think that you have to go to the church every Sunday for one hour—that hour is to be given to religion. This is an un-intelligent way to be related to religion. What has the church to do with it? Your real life is in the six days. Sunday is not your real day. You will live nonreligiously for six days, and then you go to the church just for one or two hours? Whom are you trying to deceive? Trying to deceive God that you are a churchgoer . . .

Or, if you try a little harder, then every day for twenty minutes in the morning, twenty in the evening, you do transcendental meditation. You sit with closed eyes and you repeat a mantra in a very stupid way—"Om, Om, Om"—which dulls the mind even more. To repeat a mantra me-chanically takes your intelligence away. It does not give you intelligence, it is like a lullaby.

Down the centuries, mothers have known this. Whenever a child is restless and does not want to go to sleep, the mother comes and sings a lullaby. The child feels bored, and the child cannot escape. Where to go? The mother is holding him on the bed. The only way to escape is in sleep. So he goes to sleep; he simply surrenders. He says, "It is foolish to be awake now, because she is doing such a boring thing, she goes on re-peating just a single line."

There are stories that mothers and grandmothers tell to children when they don't go to sleep. If you look into these stories, you will find a certain pattern of constant repetition. Just the other day I was reading a story told by a grandmother to a small child who does not want to go to sleep, because he does not *feel* like sleeping right now. His intelligence says that he is perfectly awake, but the grandmother is forcing him. She has other things to do—the child is not important.

Children are very puzzled, things look very absurd. When they want to sleep in the morning, everybody wants to wake them up. When they don't want to go to sleep, everybody is forcing them to sleep. They become very puzzled. What is the matter with these people? When sleep comes, good—that is intelligence. When it is not coming, it is perfectly good to be awake.

So this old grandmother is telling a story. At first the child remains interested, but by and by . . . Any intelligent child will feel bored, only a stupid child will not feel bored.

The story is:

A man goes to sleep and dreams that he is standing before a great palace. And in the palace there are one thousand and one rooms. So he goes from one room to another—one thousand rooms—then he reaches the last room. And there is a beautiful bed, so he falls on the bed, falls asleep and dreams . . . that he is standing at the door of a big palace which has one thousand and one rooms. So he goes into one thousand rooms, then he reaches the one thousand and first room. Again there is a beautiful bed, so he goes to sleep . . . and dreams that he is standing before a palace. . . . This is the way it goes!

Now, how long can the child remain alert? Just out of sheer boredom the child falls asleep. He is saying, "Now be finished!"

A mantra does the same. You repeat, "Ram, Ram . . . Om, Om . . . Allah, Allah"—or anything. You go on repeating, you go on repeating. Now you are doing two jobs: both the grandmother's and the child's. Your intelligence is like the child, and your learning of the mantra is like the grandmother. The child tries to stop you, gets interested in other things, thinks of beautiful things—beautiful women, beautiful scenes. But you catch him red-handed and bring him again to "Om, Om, Om." By and by, your inner child feels that it is futile to struggle; the inner child goes to sleep.

Yes, the mantra can give you a certain sleep: It is an autohypnotic sleep. There is nothing wrong in it if sleep is difficult for you—if you suffer from insomnia it is good. But it has nothing to do with spirituality; it is a very unintelligent way to meditate.

Then what is the intelligent way to meditate? The intelligent way is to bring intelligence into everything that you do. Walking, walk intelligently, with awareness. Eating, eat intelligently, with awareness. Do you remember ever eating intelligently? Ever thinking about what you are eating? Is it nutritious? Has it any nutritional value, or are you just stuffing yourself without any nourishment?

Have you ever watched what you do? You go on smoking. Then intelligence is needed—what are you doing? Just taking in smoke and throwing it out, and meanwhile destroying your lungs. And what are you really doing? Wasting money, wasting health. Bring intelligence in while you are smoking, while you are eating. Bring intelligence in when you go and make love to your woman or to your man. What are you doing? Have you really any love? Sometimes you make love out of habit. Then it is ugly, then it is immoral. Love has to be very conscious, only then it becomes prayer.

While making love to your woman, what exactly are you doing? Using the woman's body to throw some energy that has become too much for you? Or are you paying respect, are you loving to the woman, do you have some reverence for the woman?

I don't see it. Husbands don't respect their wives, they use them. Wives use their husbands, they don't respect them. If reverence does not arise out of love, then intelligence is missing somewhere. Otherwise you will feel tremendously grateful to the other, and your lovemaking will become a great meditation.

Whatever you are doing, bring the quality of intelligence into it. Do it intelligently: That's what meditation is.

Intelligence has to spread all over your life. It is not a Sunday thing, and you cannot do it for twenty minutes and then forget about it. Intelligence has to be just like breathing. Whatever you are doing—small, big, whatsoever, cleaning the floor—can be done intelligently or unintelligently. And you know that when you do it unintelligently there is no joy—you are doing a duty; carrying the burden of it somehow.

★   ★   ★

It happened in a church-school class of ninth-grade girls. The class was studying Christian love and what it might mean to them and their lives. They finally decided that Christian love meant "doing something lovable for someone you didn't like." Children are very intelligent. Their conclusion is perfectly right. Listen to it again. They finally decided that Christian love meant "doing something lovable for someone you didn't like."

The teacher suggested that during the week they might test out their concept. When they returned the following week, the teacher asked for reports. One girl raised her hand and said, "I've done something!"

The teacher replied, "Marvelous! What did you do?"

"Well," the girl said, "in my math class at school there is this glunky kid—"

"Glunky . . . ?"

"Yes, you know . . . glunky. She's got four heads, and she's all thumbs, and she's got three left feet, and when she comes down the hall in school, everyone says, 'Here comes that glunky kid again.' She doesn't have any friends, and nobody asks her to parties, and you know, she's just glunky."

The teacher said, "I think I know just what you mean. So what did you do?"

"Well, this glunky kid's in my math class, and she's having a tough time. I'm pretty good in math so I offered to help her with homework."

> *Whatever you are doing—small, big, whatsoever, cleaning the floor—can be done intelligently or unintelligently. And you know that when you do it unintelligently there is no joy—you are doing a duty, carrying the burden of it somehow.*

"Wonderful," said the teacher. "And what happened?"

"Well, I did help her, and it was fun, and she just couldn't thank me enough, but now, I can't get rid of her!"

If you are doing something just as a duty—you don't love it, and you are doing it just as a duty—sooner or later you will be caught in it and you will be in a difficulty about how to get rid of it. Just watch in your twenty-four-hour day, how many things you are doing that you don't derive any pleasure from, that don't help your growth. In fact, you want to get rid of them. If you are doing too many things in your life that you really want to get rid of, you are living unintelligently.

An intelligent person will make his or her life in such a way that it will have a poetry of spontaneity, of love, of joy. It is your life, and if you are not kind enough to yourself, who is going to be kind enough to you? If you are wasting your life, it is nobody else's responsibility.

I teach you to be responsible toward yourself—that is your first responsibility. Everything else comes next.

You are the very center of your world, of your existence. So, be intelligent. Bring in the quality of intelligence. And the more intelligent you become, the more capable you will be of bringing more intelligence into your life. Each single moment can become so luminous with intelligence. . . . Then there is no need for any religion, no need to meditate, no need to go to the church, no need to go to any temple, no need for anything extra. Life in its intrinsicness is intelligent. Just live totally, harmoniously, in awareness, and everything else follows beautifully. A life of celebration follows the luminousness of intelligence.

THE POETRY OF THE HEART

The intelligence of the head is not intelligence at all; it is knowledgeability. The intelligence of the heart is *the* intelligence, the only intelligence there is. The head is simply an accumulator. It is always old, it is never new, it is never original. It is good for certain purposes: For filing it is perfectly good! And in life one needs this—many things have to be remembered. The mind, the head, is a biocomputer. You can go on accumulating knowledge in it and whenever you need it you can take it out. It is good for mathematics, good for calculation, good for the day-to-day life, the marketplace. But if you think this is your whole life then you will remain stupid. You will never know the beauty of feeling and you will never know the blessings of the heart. You will never know the grace that descends only through the heart, the godliness that enters only through the heart. You will never know prayer, you will never know poetry, you will never know love.

> The intelligence of the head is not intelligence at all, it is knowledgeability. The intelligence of the heart is *the* intelligence, the only intelligence there is.

The intelligence of the heart creates poetry in your life, gives a dance to your steps, makes your life a joy, a celebration, a festivity, a laughter. It gives you a sense of humor. It makes you capable of love, of sharing. That is true life. The life that is lived from the head is a mechanical life. You become a robot—maybe very efficient. Robots are very efficient, machines are more efficient than man. You can earn much through the head, but you will not *live* much. You may have a better standard of living but you won't have any life.

Life is of the heart. Life can only grow through the heart. It is the soil of the heart where love grows, life grows, spirit grows. All that is beautiful, all that is really valuable, all that is meaningful, significant, comes through the heart. The heart is your very center, the head is just your periphery. To live in the head is to live on the circumference without ever becoming aware of the beauties and the treasures of the center. To live on the periphery is stupidity.

To live in the head is stupidity. To live in the heart and use the head whenever it is needed is intelligence. But the center, the master, is at the very core of your being.

The master is the heart, and the head is just a servant—this is intelligence. When the head becomes the master and forgets all about the heart, that is stupidity.

It is up to you to choose. Remember, the head as a slave is a beautiful slave, of much utility. But as a master it is a dangerous master and will destroy your whole life, will poison your whole life. Look around! People's lives are absolutely poisoned, poisoned by the head. They cannot feel, they are no longer sensitive, nothing thrills them. The sun rises but nothing rises in them; they look at the sun empty-eyed. The sky becomes full of the stars—the marvel, the mystery!—but nothing stirs in their hearts, no song arises. Birds sing—man has forgotten to sing. Clouds come in the sky and the peacocks dance, and man does not know how to dance. He has become a cripple. Trees bloom—and man thinks, never feels, and without feeling there is no flowering possible.

Watch, scrutinize, observe, have another look at your life. Nobody else is going to help you. You have depended on others so long; that's why you have become stupid. Now, take care; it is your own responsibility. You owe it to yourself to have a deep, penetrating look at what you are doing with your life. Is there any poetry in your heart? If it is not there, then don't waste time. Help your heart to weave and spin poetry. Is there any romance in your life or not? If there is not, then you are already in your grave.

Come out of it! Let life have something of the romantic in it, something like adventure. Explore! Millions of beauties and splendors are waiting for you. You go on moving around and around, never entering into the temple of life. The door is the heart.

The real intelligence is of the heart. It is not intellectual, it is emotional. It is not like thinking, it is like feeling. It is not logic, it is love.

Love is available only to those who go on sharpening their intelligence. Love is not for the mediocre . . . love is not for the unintelligent.

17

The unintelligent person may become a great intellectual. In fact unintelligent people try to become intellectuals; that is their way of hiding their unintelligence. Love is not for the intellectual. Love needs a totally different kind of talent—a talented heart, not a talented head.

Love has its own intelligence, its own way of seeing, perceiving, its own way of understanding life, its own way of comprehending the mystery of existence. The poet is far closer to it than the philosopher. And the mystic is exactly inside the temple. The poet is on the steps and the philosopher is just outside. At the most he can approach the driveway, but never the steps. He goes on round and round. He goes on moving around the temple, studying the outer walls of the temple, and becomes so enchanted that he forgets completely that the outer walls are not the real temple and that the deity is inside.

The poet reaches the door, but the door is so beautiful that he becomes hypnotized. He thinks he has arrived—what more can there be? The philosopher is lost in guessing what is inside. He never goes there, he simply thinks, philosophizes. The poet tries to penetrate into the mystery but gets hooked near the door. The mystic enters into the very innermost sanctum of the temple.

> Intelligence alone becomes intellectual, love alone becomes sentimentality, but a loving intelligence gives you a new kind of integrity, a new crystallization.

The way is love, and the way is a loving intelligence. When love and intelligence meet together you create the space in which all that is possible to a human being can become actual. A loving intelligence is what is needed. Intelligence alone becomes intellectual, love alone becomes sentimentality, but a loving intelligence never becomes intellectuality or sentimentality. It gives you a new kind of integrity, a new crystallization.

AN OPENNESS OF BEING

Intelligence is just an openness of being—capacity to see without prejudice, capacity to listen without interference, capacity to be with things without any a priori ideas about them—that's what intelligence is. Intelligence is an openness of being.

That's why it is so utterly different from intellectuality. Intellectuality is just the opposite of intelligence. The intellectual person is constantly carrying prejudices, information, a priori beliefs, knowledge. He cannot listen; before you have said anything, he has already concluded. Whatsoever you say has to pass through so many thoughts in his mind that by the time it reaches him it is something totally different. Great distortion happens in him, and he is very closed, almost blind and deaf. All experts, knowledgeable people, are blind.

Do you know the old story of the five blind people going to see an elephant?

A teacher was telling her students, small girls and boys, this ancient fable. She told the whole story, then she asked a small boy, "Can you tell me who the people were who went to see the elephant and then started quarreling?" She wanted to know whether the boy had listened while she was teaching the story.

And the boy stood up and said, "Yes, I know. They were the experts."

She was thinking he would answer, "They were five blind people." But the small boy said, "Those were the experts." He is far more right; yes, they were experts. All experts are blind. Expertise means you become blind to everything else. You know more and more about less and less, and then one day you arrive at the ultimate goal of knowing all about nothing. Then you are completely closed and not even a window is open; then you have become windowless.

This is unintelligence. Intelligence is to be open to wind, rain, and sun, to be open to all. Not to carry the past is intelligence, to die to the past every moment is intelligence, to remain fresh and innocent is intelligence.

Donald was driving his sports car down the main avenue when suddenly he noticed to his rear a flashing red light. It was a police car.

Quickly Donald pulled over to the side. "Officer," he blurted, "I was only doing twenty-five in a thirty-five-mile zone."

"Sir," said the officer, "I just—"

"Furthermore," interrupted Donald indignantly, "as a citizen I resent being frightened like this!"

"Please," continued the officer, "calm down, relax—"

"Relax!" shouted Donald, overwrought. "You're going to give me a traffic ticket, and you want me to relax!"

"Mister," pleaded the officer, "give me a chance to talk. I am *not* giving you a ticket."

"No?" said Donald, astonished.

"I just wanted to inform you that your right rear tire is flat."

But nobody is ready to listen to what the other is saying. Have you ever listened to what the other is saying? Before a word is uttered, you have already concluded. Your conclusions have become fixed; you are no longer liquid.

To become frozen is to become idiotic, to remain liquid is to remain intelligent. Intelligence is always flowing like a river. Unintelligence is like an ice cube, frozen. Unintelligence is always consistent, because it is frozen. It is definite, it is certain. Intelligence is inconsistent, it is flowing. It has no definition, it goes on moving according to situations. It is responsible, but it is not consistent.

Only stupid people are consistent people. The more intelligent you are, the more inconsistent you will be—because who knows about tomorrow? Tomorrow will bring its own experiences. How can you be consistent with your yesterdays? If you are dead you will be consistent. If you are alive you *have* to be inconsistent—you have grown, the world has changed, the river is flowing into new territory.

Yesterday the river was passing through a desert, today it is passing through a forest; it is totally different. Yesterday's experience should not become your definition forever; otherwise you died yesterday. One should be able to go on moving with time. One should remain a process, one should never become a thing. That is intelligence.

WHAT MAKES PEOPLE
STUPID

The mystics have compared man to a ladder. The ladder can be used for two things: You can use it to go upward, and you can use it to go downward. You use the same ladder for both purposes, only your direction changes. The ladder is the same, but the result will be totally different.

Man is a ladder between heaven and hell. That's why it is only human beings who repress, who manipulate, who kill, who try to conquer the natural flow of nature. Only human beings are stupid—and that is because they can be buddhas. Because human beings have intelligence, that's why they can be stupid. Stupidity does not mean the absence of intelligence, it simply means you have not used it. If there is no presence of intelligence you cannot call human beings stupid. You cannot call a rock stupid—a rock is a rock, there is no question of stupidity. But you can call humans stupid because with humans there is hope, a ray of great light. With the human being, a door opens toward the beyond. Man can transcend himself and he is not doing it—that's his stupidity. He can grow, and he is not growing, he is clinging to all kinds of immaturity—that is his stupidity. He goes on and on living in the past, which is no more—that is his stupidity. Or he starts projecting into the future, which is not yet—that is his stupidity.

One should live in the present with deep passion, with great love, with intensity, with awareness, and that will become your intelligence. It is the same energy—upside down it is stupidity; rearrange it, put it right, and it becomes intelligence.

Intelligence and stupidity are not separate energies. The energy that functions in harmony is intelligence, the same energy functioning in contradictions is stupidity. Man can be stupid—but don't think this is unfortunate. It appears on the surface that it is unfortunate, but hidden behind it is great glory, great splendor, which can be discovered.

But the society—the so-called religions, the state, the crowd—wants you to be stupid. Nobody wants you to be intelligent. They all condition you to remain stupid your whole life for the simple reason that stupid people are obedient. Intelligent people start thinking on their own; they start becoming individuals. They start having their own life, their own lifestyle, their own way of seeing, of being, of growing. They are no longer part of the crowd—they cannot be. They have to leave the crowd behind, only then can they grow. And the crowd feels offended; the crowd does not want anybody to be more than the "average person"— one who becomes more intelligent, more individual, more aware, will not be any longer part of the mob psychology.

You cannot force a buddha to follow stupid people, and the stupid people are many—the majority, 99.9 percent. They have a great power with them, the power of violence—and they show it whenever it is needed.

SURVIVAL OF THE FITTEST

The human being is in a dilemma for the simple reason that he is not only intelligent, he is also aware of his intelligence. That is something unique about man—his privilege, his prerogative, his glory—but it can turn very easily into his agony. Man is conscious that he is intelligent. That consciousness brings its own problems. The first problem is that it creates ego.

Ego does not exist anywhere else except in human beings, and ego starts growing as the child grows. The parents, the schools, colleges, university, they all help to strengthen the ego for the simple reason that for centuries man had to struggle to survive, and the idea has become a fixation, a deep unconscious conditioning, that only strong egos can survive in the struggle of life. Life has become just a struggle to survive. And scientists have made it even more convincing with the theory of the "survival of the fittest." So we help every child to become more and more strong in the ego, and it is there that the problem arises.

> ❧
>
> The human being is in a dilemma for the simple reason that he is not only intelligent, he is also aware of his intelligence. That is man's privilege, his prerogative, his glory—but it can turn very easily into his agony.

As the ego becomes strong it starts surrounding intelligence like a thick layer of darkness. Intelligence is light, ego is darkness. Intelligence is very delicate, ego is very hard. Intelligence is like a rose flower, ego is like a rock. And if you want to survive, they say—the so-called authorities—then you have to become rocklike, you have to be strong, invulnerable. You have to become a citadel, a closed citadel, so you cannot be attacked from outside. You have to become impenetrable.

But then you become closed. Then you start dying as far as your intelligence is concerned because intelligence needs the open sky, the wind, the air, the sun in order to grow, to expand, to flow. To remain alive it needs a constant flow; if it becomes stagnant it becomes, slowly, a dead phenomenon.

We don't allow children to remain intelligent. The first thing is that if they are intelligent they will be vulnerable, they will be delicate, they will be open. If they are intelligent they will be able to see many falsities in the society—in the state, in the church, in the educational system.

They will become rebellious. They will be individuals; they will not be cowed easily. You can crush them, but you cannot enslave them. You can destroy them, but you cannot force them to compromise.

In one sense intelligence is very soft, like a rose flower, in another sense it has its own strength. But that strength is subtle, not gross. That strength is the strength of rebellion, of a noncompromising attitude. One is ready to die, one is ready to suffer, but one is not ready to sell one's soul.

And the whole society needs slaves; it needs people who function like robots, machines. It does not want people, it wants mechanisms. Hence the whole conditioning is to make the ego strong. It serves a double purpose. First, it gives the person the feeling that now he can struggle in life. And secondly, it serves the purposes of all the vested interests. They can exploit the person; they can use him as a means to their own ends.

Hence the whole educational system rotates around the idea of ambition; it creates ambitiousness. Ambitiousness is nothing but ego. "Become the first, become the most famous. Become a prime minister or a president. Become world known, leave your mark on history." It does not teach you to live totally. It does not teach you to love totally. It does not teach you to live gracefully, it teaches you how to exploit others for your own purposes. And we think that the people who are clever are the ones who succeed. They are cunning, but we call them clever. They are not intelligent people.

An intelligent person can never use another person as a means; he will respect the other. An intelligent person will be able to see the equality of all. Yes, he will see the differences too, but differences make no difference as far as equality is concerned. He will have tremendous respect for others' freedom—he cannot exploit them, he cannot reduce them to things, he cannot make them stepping-stones to the fulfillment of some absurd desire to be the first. Hence we go on conditioning children.

But before that conditioning happens, children are immensely intelligent. It has been said by Buddha, by Lao Tzu, by Jesus, by all the awakened ones. Jesus says: Unless you are like a small child there is no hope for you. Again he says: Unless you become like small children you cannot enter into my kingdom of God. Again and again he repeats one of his most famous beatitudes: Blessed are those who are the last in this world, because they will be the first in my kingdom of God. He is teaching nonambitiousness—to be the last. He says: Blessed are the meek, for theirs is the kingdom of God—the meek, the humble, the people who are standing last in the queue. It was natural, very natural, that the society he was born in was against him, because he was destroying the very roots of their ambitiousness.

And Jews have been very ambitious people, so much so that for centuries, against all hazards, they have carried the idea in their minds that they are the chosen people of God. A thousand and one calamities have happened because of this stupid idea; if they can drop it they will be more accepted in the world. But they cannot drop it—their whole ego is involved in it. And it is an ancient ego, at least three thousand years old. Since Moses they have been carrying the idea that they are the chosen people of God. And here comes this man who says, "Be the last!" We are meant to be the first, and he says, "Be humble and meek!" And we are the chosen people! If we are humble and meek then those who are not chosen will become the first! And Jews are earthly people; they don't bother much about the other world. They are worldly: "Who knows about the other world? He is saying, 'If you are the last here you will be the first in my kingdom of God.' But where is your kingdom of God? It may be just a fiction, just a dream."

Jesus looks like a dreamer, a poet maybe. But he is destroying their very foundation. They cannot forgive him; they have not even forgiven him yet. They still carry the idea that "we are the chosen people." They have suffered much for it; the more they have suffered the stronger the idea has become—because if you have to face suffering, you have to become more and more egoistic, more rocklike, so that you can fight, struggle, so that nobody can destroy you. But they have also become very closed.

Jesus was creating an opening for them; they refused him. He was telling them to come into the open sky. He was telling them to be just ordinary: "Drop this nonsense of being special." If they had listened to Jesus their whole history would have been different, but they could not listen.

Hindus did not listen to Buddha for the same reason—Hindus are also carrying the idea they are the holiest people in the world and their land is the holiest land. Even the gods long to be born in India! No other country is so holy. And Buddha said, "This is all nonsense!" They had to reject him. Buddhism was thrown out of India. No society can tolerate such people, who are telling the truth, because they seem to sabotage the very structure of things.

But now the time has come when we have suffered enough. All over the world, in different ways, people have suffered much, and it is time to have a look at history and its stupidity and its ridiculousness and drop the whole idea of these egoistic patterns.

Watch small children and then you will see their intelligence. True, they are not knowledgeable. If you want them to be knowledgeable, then you will not think that they are intelligent. If you ask them questions that depend on information, then they will look not intelligent. But ask them *real* questions, which have nothing to do with information, which need an immediate response, and see—they are far more intelligent than you are. Of course your ego won't allow you to accept it, but if you can accept it, it will help tremendously. It will help you, it will help your children, because if you can see their intelligence you can learn much from them.

Even though the society destroys your intelligence it cannot destroy it totally; it only covers it with many layers of information. And the whole function of meditation is to take you deeper into yourself. It is a method of digging into your own being to the point when you come to the living waters of your own intelligence, when you discover the springs of your own intelligence. When you have discovered your child again, when you are reborn, then, only then will you understand why the buddhas have been emphasizing again and again that children are really intelligent.

Start watching children, their responses—not their answers but their responses. Don't ask them foolish questions, ask them something immediate which does not depend on information and see their response.

The mother was preparing little Pedro to go to a party. When she finished combing his hair she straightened his shirt collar and said, "Go now, son. Have a good time . . . and behave yourself!"

"Come on, Mother!" said Pedro. "Please decide before I leave which it is going to be!"

You see the point? The child's response is really of tremendous value. He says, "Please decide before I leave which it is going to be. If you allow me to have a good time, then I cannot behave; if you want me to behave, then I cannot have a good time." The child can see the contradiction so clearly; it may not have been apparent to the mother.

A passerby asks a boy, "Son, can you please tell me what time it is?"

"Yes, of course," replies the boy, "but what do you need it for? It's always changing!"

A new traffic sign was put in front of the school. It read: "Drive Slowly. Do Not Kill a Student!"

The following day there was another sign under it scribbled in a childish writing: "Wait for the Teacher!"

Little Pierino comes home from school with a big smile on his face.

"Well, dear, you look very happy. So you like school, do you?"

"Don't be silly, Mom," replies the boy. "We mustn't confuse the going with the coming back!"

The father was telling stories to his sons in the living room after dinner. "My great-grandfather fought in the war against Rosas in Brazie, my uncle fought in the war against the Kaiser, my grandfather fought in the war of Spain against the Republicans, and my father fought in the Second World War against the Germans."

To which the smallest son replied, "What's wrong with this family? They can't relate to anybody!"

STRIVING FOR EFFICIENCY

You will be surprised to know that your schools, colleges, and universities don't exist, in fact, to help you to become intelligent—no, not at all. I have been associated with universities as a student and then as a professor, for many years. I know the very inner structure of your educational system. It is not concerned with creating intelligence in people. Of course it wants to create efficiency—but efficiency is not intelligence, efficiency is mechanical. A computer can be very efficient, but a computer is not intelligent.

Never think that intelligence and efficiency are synonymous. Intelligence is a totally different phenomenon. Efficiency is not intelligence, it is mechanical expertise. The universities are concerned with creating efficiency so that you can be better clerks and better bureaucrats and managers. But they are not concerned with creating intelligence—in fact, they are all against intelligence. The whole structure of your educational system all over the world is to make you more and more capable of memorizing things.

Memory is a biocomputer. Intelligence is a totally different phenomenon. Intelligence arises out of meditation, intelligence arises out of rebellion. Intelligence does not arise out of memory. But your examinations only concern themselves with your memory. Whoever has a better memory is thought to be more intelligent. But it happens many times that stupid people have beautiful memories, and intelligent people are not so good as far as memory is concerned.

Thomas Edison was not good as far as memory is concerned. He invented hundreds of scientific gadgets; nobody else before him had invented so many things. Just the quantity of his inventions is enormous, unbelievable. You may not be aware that you are using Edison's inventions every day: The gramophone record, the radio, the electric bulb, the fan, the loudspeaker—all these things come from the creativity of one single person, Edison. But his memory was lousy, very sloppy, so much so that once he even forgot his own name, which is really very difficult! It is almost impossible to forget your own name. If you can forget your own name you can forget anything. He managed to do the least likely thing.

In the First World War, rationing came for the first time into existence in America, and he was standing in a queue to take his ration card. Slowly he came closer to the window. Then the last person in front of him moved and they called his name: "Thomas Alva Edison!" And he looked around as if they were calling somebody else; he looked up and down the queue . . .

One man recognized him, and said, "As far as I know, *you* are Thomas Alva Edison. Why you are looking here and there?"

Edison said, "You are right! I had completely forgotten! Many thanks that you reminded me. Yes, I am Thomas Alva Edison."

His wife used to have to keep everything in order because his whole room was in constant chaos—thousands of papers, research papers—and whenever he wanted to find something it would take days to figure out where it was. He kept forgetting everything. He might have invented something and would start inventing it again. And his wife would remind him, "You have done it! It is already in the market!"

He used to keep loose papers around, and would go on writing down whatever thought came to his mind. Then those loose papers would be lost here and there. His wife told him, "It would be better if you would keep a notebook."

He said, "That's a beautiful idea! Why did it never occur to me?" But then he lost the whole notebook! He said, "Look what happened when I followed your suggestion. With loose papers at least one thing was good—once in a while I would lose a few notes, but not all of them. Now all my notes are lost!"

Albert Einstein was not a man who had a good memory. He failed many exams in school simply because he could not memorize anything. This greatest mathematician of all the ages, and for ages to come, was incapable of counting small amounts of money. He would have to count again and again. Once he was traveling in a bus. He gave the conductor some money; the change was returned to him. He counted it once, twice, thrice, and each time the result was different, so he started counting the fourth time.

The conductor was watching and he said, "What is the matter with you? Don't you know figures? Thrice you have counted, now you are counting a fourth time! Don't you know how to count change?"

Einstein said, "Yes, I am a little lousy in math."

This man who had worked out the greatest mathematics possible was incapable of counting small amounts of money. He would go into his bathroom and would not come out for hours because he would forget where he was and that he should come out. One of my friends, Doctor Ram Manohar Lohia, went to see him. He told me, "I had to wait six hours because he was in the bathroom! And his wife kept apologizing again and again. She said, 'He is in the bathroom, he is still in the bathroom.' I said, 'But what is he doing in the bathroom?' The wife said, 'Nobody knows . . . but if you disturb him he becomes very angry—he starts throwing things! But he always forgets; whenever he goes in there he forgets to come out. Now we have to wait until whenever he comes. When he starts to feel hungry or thirsty or something, then he will remember.' "

Doctor Lohia asked, "But what is he doing in there?"

The wife said, "I have also been curious about that for all these years. In the beginning I used to peep through the keyhole—what is he doing? He sits in the bathtub playing with soap bubbles! When I asked him, 'What are you doing?' he said, 'Don't disturb me—never disturb me, because it is in playing with soap bubbles that I have discovered the theory of relativity. It is through playing with soap bubbles that I came to understand that the universe is expanding just like a soap bubble. It goes on expanding and one day it will burst—just like a soap bubble!' "

> *Memory and intelligence come from different sources. Memory is part of the mind—intelligence is part of no-mind. Intelligence is part of your consciousness, and memory is part of your brain.*

If you look down the ages you will find thousands of geniuses with very bad memories and thousands of people who had tremendous memories with no intelligence at all—because memory and intelligence come from different sources. Memory is part of the mind—intelligence is part of no-mind. Intelligence is part of your consciousness, and memory is part of your brain. The brain can be trained—that's what the universities go on doing. All your examinations are tests for your memory, not for your intelligence. The universities give you the wrong impression—as if memory is intelligence. It is not.

This whole educational system exists to destroy intelligence or to divert you from intelligence toward memory. Memory is useful, utilitarian. Intelligence is dangerous; it has no utility for the status quo, it has no utility for the vested interests. Intelligent people have always proved to be difficult people just because of their intelligence. They cannot bow down to any stupid thing. And our society is full of superstitions, stupidities—all kinds of nonsense prevails

in the name of religion, in the name of politics, in the name of literature, art.

REPRESSION AND MANIPULATION

Each child is distracted, is diverted. Hence there is so much stupidity. It is
really a miracle how a few people have escaped from this prison—a Buddha, a Zarathustra, a Lao Tzu, a Jesus, a Pythagoras . . . very few people. It
is almost impossible to escape from this prison because the prison is all
around, and it starts from the very beginning. From your very childhood
you are conditioned to be a prisoner—a Christian, a Hindu, a Mohammedan. And when you are prisoners of churches, nations, races, then
naturally there is going to be violence.

No animal is as violent as man. Animals kill but they kill only when
they are hungry, otherwise not. Man is the only animal who enjoys
killing for no reason at all, as if killing in itself is a blissful activity.

One day in a restaurant a lion and a hare entered. The manager
was shocked; he could not believe his eyes. A great silence fell
over the restaurant. Many people were there eating, talking, gos-
siping; all became absolutely silent. What was happening? The
manager rushed to the new customers. Somehow he managed
to stammer to the hare, "What would you like, sir?"

The hare asked for coffee. The manager asked, "And what
would your friend like to have?"

The hare laughed and he said, "Do you think if he were
hungry I would be here? He is not hungry; otherwise he would
have eaten his breakfast and I would be gone! We can be together only when he is not hungry."

A lion won't kill if he is not hungry. It is only man who kills for no
reason at all—for stupid ideas. One can understand—if somebody is

hungry, one can understand. But one cannot understand Hiroshima and Nagasaki—destroying a hundred thousand people within three minutes, just for the sheer joy of destruction.

This is happening because we have not allowed man's intelligence to flower. And whenever it has happened in any society that intelligence is allowed a little freedom, that society has become weaker than other societies. It happened in India: India remained a slave for two thousand years for many reasons. One of the reasons was the great revolution that was brought by Krishna, Patanjali, Saraha, Mahavira, Buddha. These people brought such a great revolution, such a radical change in the consciousness of India, that many people were released from the bondage of stupidity; a great intelligence was released. The result was that the intelligent people stopped killing, they became nonviolent; they refused to be recruited into the army. Buddhists and Jains refused to be recruited into the army, the Brahmins refused to be recruited into the army. Now this was the cream, and the cream refused to fight. Then very stupid countries and very ordinary people—Huns, Turks, Moghuls, who were backward in every possible way—overran the country. And because the most intelligent people of the younger generation were no longer interested in killing and violence, there was no resistance, no fight. These people conquered the country—a big country was conquered by very small countries. For two thousand years India remained in slavery for that simple reason.

The same thing happened in Athens. Socrates, Plato, Aristotle, Pythagoras, Heraclitus . . . these were the people who released great intelligence, and a climate was created of freedom, of free thinking. It was one of the most beautiful phenomena that was happening on the earth, and it was destroyed by stupid people, barbarians. The whole Greek civilization disappeared.

My own suggestion is that unless we create a world government, intelligence cannot be allowed. The time has come for a world government. National governments are no longer needed: They are things of the past, they are part of our stupid past. Nations are no longer needed, only a world government. And if there is a world government it will have a totally different quality.

Armies will have to be reduced, because there will be no question of fighting with anybody. Now seventy percent of the world's money, wealth, resources goes to the military and military weapons—seventy percent! Only thirty percent is left for other purposes. That means seventy percent of our energy is devoted to killing, to being violent, to being destructive.

A world government is an absolute necessity to save humanity. And the quality of the world government will be totally different because it won't need great armies; just small police forces will be enough. It will take care of all things like the post office, the railway, the airplanes, et cetera—but they are not destructive; they serve people. And once the armies disappear from the world, great intelligence will be released—because the army is destructive of intelligence. It recruits the healthiest people and destroys their minds, because a real soldier is possible only if the person becomes absolutely mechanical.

Man kills for no reason. Man tries to repress rather than to understand, to manipulate rather than to relate, because to relate with somebody needs great understanding.

Manipulation needs no understanding. Repression is easy, very easy—any fool can do it. That's why if you go to the monasteries you will find all kinds of repressions and you will find all kinds of fools gathered together there. I have never come across intelligent monks and nuns; if they are intelligent they will not be monks and nuns anymore. They will renounce that nonsense, they will come out of their so-called religious prisons. But repression needs no wisdom; it simply needs a powerful ego, so you can go on suppressing everything into the unconscious. But whatever you suppress will have to be suppressed again and again—and still it will never be eliminated. It will become more and more powerful as you grow older because you will become weaker. The suppressor will become weaker and the suppressed will remain fresh and young, because it has never been used.

The real problem arises in old age when suppression starts exploding and creates all kinds of ugliness. It is five thousand years of suppression that is creating all our neuroses, all our perversions. Suppress sex and you will become more sexual; your whole life will be colored with sex. You will think always in terms of sexuality and nothing else. Suppress sex and the ugly institution of prostitution will arise, is *bound* to arise. The more suppressive a society is, the more prostitutes will be found there; the proportion is always the same. You can count your nuns and monks and you can know by counting them how many male and female prostitutes will be in the country. It will be exactly the same number because nature keeps a balance. And perversions . . . because sexual energy will find its ways, its own ways. Either it will create neurosis or hypocrisy. Both are ill states. The poor will become neurotic and the rich will become hypocrites.

It is said that when Moses in his rage smashed the tablets of the Ten Commandments, everybody rushed to grab a piece.

Of course the rich and the politicians were the first. They got all the good pieces on which were inscribed, "Commit adultery," "lie," "steal." The poor and all the rest got only the pieces that said, "Thou shalt not," "Thou shalt not."

Repression creates cunningness. You lose authenticity, you lose naturalness, spontaneity. You lose truth. You start lying to others, you start lying to yourself. You start finding ways to lie and to go on lying. And a single lie will need a thousand other lies to protect it, to support it.

THE SIN OF DISOBEDIENCE

It is said that when Henry Thoreau came out of the university, Emerson gave a big party to celebrate the occasion. And he told the participants, "I am giving this party not because Thoreau has attained great knowledge in the university but because he has been able to come back from the university and he is still intelligent. The university has not been able to destroy his intelligence. The university has failed, that's why I am giving this party! I respect this young man for the simple reason that he has escaped from the whole cunning strategy that is our education."

Intelligence simply means the ability to respond, because life is a flux. You have to be aware and to see what is demanded of you, what is the challenge of the situation. The intelligent person behaves according to the situation, and the stupid behaves according to the ready-made answers. Whether those answers come from Buddha, Christ, or Krishna, he always carries "scriptures" around himself. He is afraid to depend on himself. The intelligent person depends on his own insight. He trusts his own being. He loves and respects himself. The unintelligent person respects others.

And you can see the point—why are the vested interests interested in creating stupidity? Because that is the only way they can get respect. No parents really want their children to be intelligent, because if the children are intelligent they are rebellious, too; they are disobedient, too. Obedience has been imposed on you as a great value—it is not. It is one of the basic causes of the destruction of your intelligence.

I am not saying be disobedient. I am simply saying that when you feel like being obedient, be obedient; when you feel like being disobedient, be true to yourself. Your only responsibility is toward yourself and nobody else.

An intelligent person takes risks. He will be ready to die rather than to compromise. Of course, he will not fight about unnecessary things, he will not fight about nonessentials—but as far as the essentials are concerned he is not going to be obedient.

> The intelligent person behaves according to the situation, and the stupid behaves according to the ready-made answers, he always carries "scriptures." The intelligent person depends on his own insight. He trusts his own being.

But you have obeyed even about the essentials. What is your belief in God? You have simply obeyed others. What do *you* know about God?

You have simply obeyed; you have followed your parents, and they followed their parents. Parents are happy with unintelligent children because they are obedient—they *have* to be obedient. The children come to know one thing, that whatever they do is bound to be wrong, so it is better to listen to the parents' advice.

For thousands of years every society has been telling children, "Respect your parents," because they are afraid of children—they may not respect their parents. And I am not saying to disrespect your parents. I am simply saying that you must first respect yourself. Out of that respect, you can respect your parents, your teachers—you can respect everybody. But if you don't respect yourself, your respect for anybody else is going to be false; deep down there will be hatred. Each child hates his parents . . . deep down he feels, "The parents are my enemies." He can see how his intelligence is being crippled.

After putting her two children to bed one night, a young mother changed into a ragged blouse and an old pair of slacks and proceeded to wash her hair. All during the shampoo she could hear the children growing wilder and noisier. Finishing as hurriedly as possible, she wrapped a large towel around her head, stormed into their room, and put them back to bed with a stern warning to stay there. As she left, she heard the two-year-old say to his sister in a trembling voice, "Who was *that*?"

This is intelligence!

But the society is not interested in intelligent people. It is not interested in seekers, it is interested in soldiers. It wants to create soldiers. And unless you are stupid you cannot be a good soldier. The greater you are in your stupidity the better, as far as being a soldier is concerned.

As the last soldier was about to jump from the airplane he panicked, grabbed hold of his sergeant and said, "What happens if my second parachute doesn't open, either?"

"Don't worry," said the sergeant with a smile. "Just come back and I will give you a new one!"

Life is a beautiful journey if it is a process of constant learning, exploration. Then it is excitement every moment, because every moment you are opening a new door, every moment you are coming in contact with a new mystery.

The word *disciple* means one who learns, and *discipline* means the process of learning. But the word has been prostituted. Now *discipline* means obedience. They have turned the whole world into a Boy Scout camp. High above there is somebody who knows—you need not learn, you have simply to obey. They have turned the meaning of *discipline* into its very opposite.

Learning automatically consists of doubting, of questioning, of being skeptical, of being curious—not of being a believer certainly, because a believer never learns. But they have used the word for thousands of years in this way. And it is not only one word that they have prostituted, they have prostituted many words. Beautiful words have become so ugly in the hands of the vested interests that you cannot even imagine the original meaning of the word . . . thousands of years of misuse.

They want everybody to be disciplined the way people are disciplined in the army. You are ordered and you have to do it without asking why. This is not the way of learning! And from the very beginning they have imposed stories on the minds of people—for example that the first sin committed was disobedience. Adam and Eve were expelled from the Garden of Eden because they disobeyed.

I have looked at it in thousands of ways, but I don't see that Adam and Eve committed any sin or any crime. They were simply exploring. You are in a garden and you start exploring the fruits and flowers and what is edible and what is not edible.

And God is responsible, because he prohibited them from two trees. He indicated the trees: "You should not approach these two trees. One is the tree of wisdom, and the other is the tree of eternal life." Just think, if you were Adam and Eve—was not God himself tempting you to go to these two trees? And those two trees were of wisdom and of eternal life—why should God be against them? If he were really a father, one who loved you, he might have pointed to them, saying, "This is a poisonous tree, don't eat from it." Or, "This is the tree of death; if you eat anything from it you will die." But these two trees are perfectly good! Eat as much as you can, because to be wise and to have eternal life is absolutely right.

Every father would want his children to have wisdom and eternal life. This father seems to be absolutely loveless. Not only loveless but, as the devil said to Eve, "He has prevented you from these two trees. Do you know the reason? The reason is that if you eat from these two trees you will be equal to him, and he is jealous. He does not want you to become divine. He does not want you to become gods, full of wisdom and eternal life."

I cannot see that the devil's argument has any flaw in it. It is absolutely right. In fact, he is the first benefactor of humanity. Without him, perhaps there would have been no humanity—no Gautam Buddha, no Kabir, no Christ, no Zarathustra, no Lao Tzu . . . just buffaloes and donkeys, all eating grass, chewing grass contentedly. And God would have been very happy, that his children are very obedient!

But this obedience is poison, pure poison. The devil must be counted as the first revolutionary of the world, and the first man to think in terms of evolution, of wisdom, of eternal life.

JUST FOLLOWING ORDERS

All over the world, in every army, they are turning millions of people into machines—of course, in such a way that you don't understand what is going on. Their methodology is very indirect.

What does it mean that thousands of people every morning are marching, following orders: "Right turn, left turn, move forward, move backward." For what is all this circus going on? And for years it goes on.

This is to destroy your intelligence. For years continuously you go on following any kind of stupid order, meaningless, every day in the morning, every day in the evening—and you are not supposed to ask why. You just have to do it, to do it as perfectly as possible; there is no need for you to understand why. And when a person goes through such a training for years, the natural effect is that he stops asking why.

The questioning attitude is the very base of all intelligence. The moment you stop asking why, you have stopped growing as far as intelligence is concerned.

> The questioning attitude is the very base of all intelligence. The moment you stop asking why, you have stopped growing as far as intelligence is concerned.

It happened in the Second World War . . .

A retired army man . . . he had fought in the First World War and he was honored; he was a brave man. And now almost twenty-five years had passed. He had a small farm and lived silently.

He was going from the farm to the town with a bucketful of eggs, and a few people in a restaurant, just jokingly, played a trick on the poor old army man. One of the men in the restaurant shouted, "Attention!" and the man dropped the bucket and stood in the position of attention.

It had been twenty-five years since he had gone through the training. But the training had gone into the bones, into the blood, into the marrow; it had become part of the unconscious. He completely forgot what he was doing—it happened almost autonomously, mechanically.

He was very angry. But those people said, "Your anger is not right, because we can call out any word we want. Who is telling you to follow it?"

He said, "It is too late for me to decide whether to follow it or not to follow it. My whole mind functions like a machine. Those twenty-five years simply disappeared. *Attention* only means attention. You destroyed my eggs, and I am a poor man . . ."

But this is being done all over the world. And not only today; from the very beginning armies have been trained not to use their intelligence but to follow orders.

You have to understand one thing very clearly: To follow an order and to understand a thing are two diametrically opposite things. If, by understanding, your intelligence feels satisfied and you do something out of that, you are not following an order from the outside; you are following your own intelligence.

I am reminded of another incident in the First World War. In Berlin, a German professor of logic was recruited into the army. There was a shortage of soldiers, and everybody who was physically able was asked to volunteer. Otherwise, they were forcing people to join the army. All the societies, all the nations, all the cultures, have taken it for granted that the individual exists for them, not vice versa.

To me, just the opposite is the case: The society exists for the individual, the culture exists for the individual, the nation exists for the individual. Everything else can be sacrificed, but the individual cannot be sacrificed for anything. Individuality is the very flowering of existence—nothing is higher. But no culture, no society, no civilization is ready to accept that simple truth.

The professor was forced to volunteer for the army. He said, "I am not a man who can fight. I can argue, I am a logician. If you need somebody to argue with the enemies I am ready, but fighting is not my business. It is barbarous to fight."

But nobody listened, and finally he was brought to the parade grounds. The parade started, and the commander said, "Left turn." Everybody turned left, but the professor remained standing as he was standing.

The commander was a little worried: "What is the matter? Perhaps the man is deaf." So he shouted loudly, "Now turn to the left again!" All the people turned to the left again, but that man remained standing as if he had not heard anything. Forward, backward . . . all the orders were given and everybody followed. That man remained just standing in his place.

He was a well-known professor; even the commander knew him. He could not be treated just like any other soldier, he inspired a certain respect. Finally, when the parade ended and everybody returned to where they had started, the commander went to the professor and asked, "Is there some problem with your ears? Can't you hear?"

He said, "I can hear."

"But then," the commander said, "why did you remain standing? Why did you not follow the orders?"

He said, "What is the point? When everybody finally has to come back to the same state, after all this movement going forward and backward, left and right, what have they gained?"

The commander said, "It is not a question of gaining, it is a question of training!"

But he said, "I don't need any training. You come to the same place after doing all kinds of stupid things, which I don't see any point in. Can you explain to me why I should turn left and not right?"

The commander said, "Strange, no soldier asks such questions."

The professor said, "I am not a soldier, I am a professor. I have been forced to be here, but you cannot force me to do things against my intelligence."

The commander went to the higher authorities and said, "What to do with this man? He may ruin the others—because everybody is laughing at me, and everybody is saying, 'Professor, you did great!' I cannot tackle that man. He asks such questions, and each thing has to be explained: 'Unless I understand it, unless my intelligence supports it, I am not going to do it.' "

The commander in chief said, "I know the man. He is a great logician. His whole life's training is in questioning everything. I will take care of him, don't be worried."

He called the professor to his office and said, "I am sorry, but we cannot do anything. You have been recruited; the country needs soldiers. But I will give you some work that will not create any difficulty for you and will not create any difficulty for others. You come with me to the army mess."

He took the professor there, and showed him a big pile of green peas. He told the professor, "Sit down here. You can sort out the big peas on one side and the small peas on the other side. In an hour I will come to see how things are progressing."

After an hour he came back. The professor was sitting there and the peas were also sitting there, in the same place. He said, "What is the matter? You have not even started."

The professor said, "For the first and for the last time, I want you all to understand that unless you explain to me . . . Why should I sort out the peas? My intelligence feels insulted by you. Am I an idiot, to sort these peas? What is the need? Moreover, there are other difficulties. Sitting here, I thought that perhaps there could be some need, but there are questions which have to be decided: There are peas that are big and there are peas that are small, but there are peas of many other sizes. Where are they going to go? You have not given me any criteria."

Orders, disciplines, guidelines—these have been used by people who wanted to dominate you, by people who wanted to dictate their terms, to enforce their ideas on other people's lives. I call all such people great criminals. To impose their ideas on somebody, to enforce some ideal, some mold, is violence, sheer violence. They are being destructive.

MIND—A PANDORA'S BOX

Man's mind is a Pandora's box.

It contains the whole of evolution from the lowest creature to the highest genius. They are all living together in man's mind simultaneously, they are all contemporaries. It is not that something is past, something is present, something is future: As far as mind is concerned everything is simultaneous, contemporary.

It has to be understood very clearly because without understanding it the question of divisive belief systems and fanaticism will remain unresolved. The idiot is in you, and so is the genius. Of course, the idiot is much more powerful because it has a longer history, and the genius is a very still, small voice. From Khomeini to Einstein you are spread; and the trouble is that Khomeini is in the majority, much more in you than Albert Einstein, who is in a very poor minority.

Think of man's mind as a pyramid. The base is made up of Khomeinis, millions of Khomeiniacs, and as you go upward there are fewer and fewer people. At the peak they are not in millions, not in billions, only in dozens—and at the very peak, perhaps there is a single individual.

> The idiot is in you, and so is the genius. Of course, the idiot is much more powerful because it has a longer history, and the genius is a very still, small voice.

But remember that the difference between Khomeini and Einstein is not of quality, it is only of quantity, because part of Khomeini is Albert Einstein, and the major part of Albert Einstein is also Khomeini.

Recently the results of a three-year-long study of Albert Einstein's brain were published. It took three years just to count the cells of his brain. There are millions of cells in every brain doing different kinds of specific work: It is a very miraculous world.

How a certain cell functions in a certain way is still not known. A certain cell thinks, a certain cell dreams, a certain cell poetizes, a certain cell paints. What makes the difference between these groups of cells? They are all alike as far as chemistry and physiology is concerned; there seems to be no difference at all. But there are cells which think, there are cells which imagine, there are cells which are mathematical, and there are cells which are philosophical. It is a whole world.

Three years counting the cells of Albert Einstein's brain—the result is very significant. A certain kind of cell has been found in his brain—twenty-seven percent more than in the average brain. That certain kind of cell has only one function: to feed, nourish, the thinking cells. It has no direct function, it is a nourishment to the thinking cells. And this nourishing cell has been found to be twenty-seven percent more numerous in Einstein than in the ordinary, average man.

Now the difference is of quantity, it is not a qualitative difference: Those extra twenty-seven percent of cells can be grown in you. And why only twenty-seven? Two hundred and seventy percent more can be grown, because it is well known and an established fact how those cells grow.

In white mice they have been growing all kinds of cells. If the white mouse is given more things to play with, he starts growing those nourishing cells, because he has to think. If you put him in a maze and he has to find the way through it—if you put him in a box where food is hidden somewhere and he has to find the way through all kinds of labyrinths to reach the food, and he has to remember the ways that he has followed—of course a certain kind of thinking has started. And the more he thinks, the greater his need for the nourishing cell.

Nature provides you whatever you need. Whatever you have is not given by any god, by fate; it has been created by your need. But one thing out of this whole research is very shocking and shattering: that the difference between Einstein and Khomeini is only of quantity. And that quantity also is not something special, it can be created: old Khomeini just has to start playing chess, cards . . . Of course he won't, but if he starts playing chess and cards and other things, he will have to think.

Religions kill this very nourishing cell because they tell you to believe. Believing means: Don't think, don't play with ideas. Don't try to find out on your own. Jesus has already found it, Buddha has already said it—why should you be unnecessarily concerned? Then naturally that part that makes a man an Einstein does not develop: You remain average. And average means the basement of humanity.

Hence, I call man's mind a Pandora's box. And for another reason also—because whatever has happened in evolution has left its traces within you. You are still afraid of darkness—that fear must be millions of years old; it has nothing to do with the modern world. In fact it is difficult in a place like New York to find a dark corner, everything is so lighted. People may not be enlightened, but places are!

Why this fear of darkness? Because in modern life you don't come across darkness in any fearful way. If you meet darkness at all it is soothing, relaxing, rejuvenating. Rather than being afraid of it you should have a certain love for it. But the very idea of loving darkness seems absurd. Somewhere deep down in your heart is still the caveman who was afraid

> Believing means: Don't think, don't play with ideas. Don't try to find out on your own. Jesus has already found it, Buddha has already said it—why should you be unnecessarily concerned?

of darkness. The fear of darkness comes from those days when ways to create fire had not been discovered. Those were the days of darkness, and darkness became almost synonymous with evil. Everywhere evil is painted as dark, black. Darkness became synonymous with death. Everywhere death is painted as black.

The reason is very clear: Before man learned how to create fire, night was the most dangerous time. If you survived one night you had done something really great, because in the night all the wild animals were ready to attack you. You could not sleep, you had to remain awake—just the fear of the wild animals was enough to keep you awake. And still they would attack in darkness, and man was helpless.

So darkness became evil, bad, and synonymous with death. And the fear has entered so deep in the heart that it remains even today, when darkness has gone through a complete transformation . . . Neither do wild animals attack you in the dark, nor does darkness bring any evil or death to you. It only brings soothing sleep, takes away all the tiredness of the day; makes you again young, alive, full of energy, ready to meet tomorrow's morning sun. But our attitude remains the same. So is the case with everything.

In the past, throughout the whole of evolution, man had to become part of a certain group, organization, society, tribe, for the simple reason that alone, he was so helpless. Alone, and the whole wilderness against you—it was difficult to face it. Together, with a crowd, you felt more protected, more secure.

You have to remember that man is the most weak and helpless animal in the world, and because of this helplessness and weakness our whole civilization and culture has grown. So don't think of it as a curse; it has proved a great, the greatest, blessing. Lions cannot create a society, lions cannot create culture because a lion has no need of the group. He alone is powerful enough. Sheep move in groups; lions don't move in groups. Each lion has its own territorial imperative. They have a specific technique to declare their territory. All the animals have it—they piss on a certain area and its smell makes others aware that this is the boundary line, the fence. Outside it, everything is okay; just a single step inside the territory and there is danger.

Lions like to be alone for the simple reason that they are enough for any enemy. Now if you think about man . . . his body is not so strong as that of an animal. His nails are not so strong that he can kill any animal just with his nails. His teeth are not so strong that he can eat the raw meat of an animal killed with his own hands. Neither can he kill with his hands nor can he eat raw meat directly with his teeth. All his limbs are weaker than those of other animals. He cannot run with a horse or with a dog, or with a bull, or with a wolf, or with a deer—he is just a nobody! It is good that these people don't participate in your Olympic races; otherwise your great runners would just look silly. You cannot move like monkeys from one tree to another. They go on jumping from one tree to another tree for miles; they need not touch the ground. You cannot fight even with a monkey.

It has to be accepted that man is the weakest animal on the earth. And this is the foundation of his whole behavior, his commitments, his groupings. He has to be part of something bigger than himself; only then does he feel safe.

He had to invent all kinds of weapons. No animal has bothered to invent weapons. There is no need; their hands, their teeth, their nails, are enough. From the earliest days man had to invent weapons—first made of stones, rocks, then slowly with metals. Then he had to admit that even with a weapon in his hand he could not fight with a lion or an animal at close quarters. He had to invent arrows—that is, shooting from a distance—because coming close was dangerous. You may have a weapon but it won't be of much use against an elephant. He will take you and your weapon both together and throw you half a mile away. Shooting from a distance in some way or other became necessary.

That's how we have arrived at nuclear weapons. Now we have taken the man completely out of it; you just push a button and a rocket shoots. You need not know where the rocket is; it goes on its programmed course. It will reach the Kremlin or it will reach the White House; that program is inbuilt. Who pushes the button does not matter; he can be miles away. He has to be miles away because after all the man is not a pope, he is fallible: Things can backfire. The rockets may be somewhere in Texas and the buttons, the switches, may be somewhere in the White House.

Man has created distance between himself and the enemy, and finally he had to create distance between himself and the weapon too, because the weapon became too dangerous. To keep it close is taking an unnecessary risk.

But everything has grown in a very logical way. Man has become the conqueror of all the animals. Only in this sense can it be said, "Blessed are the meek for they shall inherit the kingdom of the earth." They have inherited it only in this sense, but in no other, spiritual sense. Man's weakness has proved his strength.

> ≋
>
> Whenever animals have to encounter something, they know exactly what they have to do, hence thinking does not grow. Man was left without any solutions, with immense problems surrounding him—he *had* to think.

Man had to think, he had to work things out. There were so many problems and he had no natural way to find out solutions—hence, thinking. Thinking simply means you are faced with a problem and nature has not given you the clue to it. All the animals are provided with clues. They never face any problem. Whenever they have to encounter something, they know exactly what they have to do; hence thinking does not grow. Man was left without any solutions, with immense problems surrounding him—he *had* to think.

Over millions of years his thinking cells became more and more efficient. But along the way he was gathering all kinds of dust, all kinds of fears.

It was necessary, it could not be avoided; but the trouble is that time has passed, you have passed through that way, but the dust is still clinging to you.

Now man can be alone. Now there is no need for him to be fanatically committed to any religious group, any political ideology—Christianity, Hinduism, Mohammedanism, communism, fascism—there is no need. But the majority consists of idiots. They go on reliving their past again and again. It is said that history repeats itself—that is true as far as ninety-nine percent of humanity is concerned; it can't be otherwise. It has to repeat itself because these people go on clinging to their past, and they go on doing the same things again and again.

They cluster in groups—and this has to be a commitment, because otherwise why should the group take on the burden of including you? You have to pay something in return. Why should the group bother about your safety? You have to do something for the group—that is your commitment. You say, "I am ready to die for you. If you are ready to die for me, I am ready to die for you." It is a simple bargain.

And why are they fanatically committed? They have to be fanatically committed because if they start being conscious, alert, they will see what an idiotic thing it is.

There is no need to belong to Adolf Hitler's Nazi party. But a country like Germany—one of the most educated, cultured, sophisticated; the country that has given the longest list of thinkers and philosophers to the world—falls victim to an utter idiot. And a man like Martin Heidegger, one of the most important philosophers of his age, perhaps the most important, was a follower of Adolf Hitler. One cannot believe it. It is simply inconceivable that a man like Martin Heidegger, who has no comparison anywhere in the world . . . all of his contemporaries look like pygmies in comparison. Heidegger's thinking was so complex that he could never finish any of his books. He would start, he would write the first part, and then the whole world would be waiting for the second part to appear. And it would never appear for the simple reason that by the end of the first part he had created so many problems for himself that now he did not know where to move, where to go, what to do, or how to resolve it all. He simply kept silent and started another book!

And that's what he did his whole life. The first part appears, then the second part, the third part, is missing, no book is complete. But even those incomplete pieces are simply miracles of the mind. The fineness of his logic and the depth of his approach. . . . But even this man could not see that Adolf Hitler was a madman. He was also fanatically committed to Adolf Hitler.

From where does this urge to be fanatically committed come?

It comes from your doubt. You cannot really convince yourself that what you are doing is right, so you have to overdo it. You have to shout loudly so that you can hear; you have to convince others so that in turn you can be convinced. You have to convert others, so that seeing you have converted thousands of people you are at ease: There must be some truth in what you are saying; otherwise, why are so many people convinced? You can be a fool, but so many people can't be foolish.

Just think of Adolf Hitler: He can think of himself as a fool, but what about Martin Heidegger? He has convinced Martin Heidegger; now no other proof is needed. This man is proof enough that what he is saying is right. This is a reciprocal process, a vicious circle. You become more convinced by having more fanatically committed people around you, and because you become more convinced you start gathering more people around you.

Adolf Hitler says in his autobiography that it does not matter what you are saying—whether it is right or wrong, true or false—just go on repeating it with conviction. Nobody is bothered about its rationality and logic. How many people in the world understand what logic is, what rationality is? Just go on repeating yourself with force, with emphasis. Those people are in search of conviction, not in search of truth. They are in search of somebody who knows it. And how can they feel that you know it if you say *if* and *but, perhaps . . .?*

That's why the Jain mystic Mahavira could not gather many followers in India—because he started every one of his statements with *perhaps.* He was right, he was absolutely correct—but that is not the way to find followers. Even those who were following by and by disappeared: "Perhaps . . . this man is talking about 'perhaps'? *Perhaps* there is a God?" Can you gather a following committed to your *perhaps*? They want certainty, they want a guarantee. Mahavira was too wise a man for all those idiots. He behaved with people as if they were capable of the same level of understanding he had.

What he was saying would be understood by Albert Einstein, because what Albert Einstein says is also with a *perhaps*. That's the whole meaning of the theory of relativity: Nothing can be said with certainty because everything is only relative, nothing is certain. Can you say this is light? It is only relative. In comparison to a brighter light it may look very dim. In comparison to a light that is a million times brighter, it may look like just a black hole, just a darkness. What is darkness? Less light. There are animals, cats, moving in the house in the night perfectly well. In your house, even somebody else's cat can move better than you can move in the darkness. You will stumble, but the cat has eyes that can catch dimmer rays of light.

The owl only sees in the night; the day is too bright. The owl needs sunglasses; without sunglasses he cannot see, the day is too bright. When it is morning to you, it is evening to the owl. Now what is what? Think of the owl, then you will understand the meaning of *perhaps*—perhaps it is evening; as far as the owl is concerned perhaps it is morning. As the night grows darker, the owl sees better. In the middle of the night it is the middle of the day for the owl.

Things are relative; hence to say anything with certainty is to show your stupidity. That's why Mahavira used a strange approach for the first time in the history of man, twenty-five centuries before Albert Einstein. His word for *perhaps* is *syat*. His philosophy became known as *syatvad*, "the philosophy of perhaps." You could ask any question; he would never answer you with certainty. You might have come with some certainty; by the time you left him you would be more uncertain. Now, who wants to follow such a man?

Adolf Hitler is going to be followed because he takes uncertainty, which was like a wound, out of you. You are trembling inside; you don't know what this life is all about. But *somebody* knows, and you can follow that somebody. You are relieved of a great burden of uncertainty. All that is needed from your side is a fanatical belief.

The fanatical belief serves both sides. The leader needs it because he himself is just like you, trembling deep inside; he knows nothing. All he knows is that he can shout better than you, that he is more articulate than you, that he at least can pose as if he knows—that he is a good actor, a very refined hypocrite. But deep down he knows that he is trembling. He needs a great following, which will help him to get rid of his fear, which will convince him that he knows.

I have heard that it happened that a journalist died and reached the gates of paradise. Journalists are not supposed to go there; how it happened I don't know. The gatekeeper looked at him and said, "Are you a journalist?"

He said, "Of course, and as a press reporter I am allowed everywhere. Let me in."

The gatekeeper said, "There is a difficulty. In the first place, in paradise we don't have any newspaper because no news happens here—no crime, no drunkards, no rape. There are only saints, dried up, frozen from eternity till eternity. So what news is there? Still, we have a quota of ten journalists, but that has been full from the very beginning. You will have to go to the other gate on the other side of the road."

The journalist said, "Can you do a little favor for me? I will leave after twenty-four hours, but just give me a chance, at least a tour. If you cannot allow me a permanent, residential green card, you can let me have a twenty-four-hour tour. That is not too much to ask. Since I come from so far away, have mercy on me. And give me one promise: If I can convince one of those ten journalists to go to hell in my place, then will you let me stay here?"

The gatekeeper said, "No problem. If you can convince somebody to go to the other place, you can be in his place. It makes no difference to us; the quota is ten."

The man said, "Then just give me twenty-four hours."

He went in and he started talking to everybody, whomever he met. "Have you heard that in hell they are going to start a new daily newspaper, the biggest that has ever been tried? And they are in need of a chief editor, editorial staff, and all kinds of journalists. Weekly editors, and literary editors . . . haven't you heard?"

The others said, "We have not heard anything, but that is great. In this rotten place, only one issue of a newspaper was published, way back in the beginning of time, but since then nothing has happened. So we go on reading the first issue again and again, what else to do? This new paper sounds great!" All ten journalists became agitated. The next day, after twenty-four hours, the journalist went back to the gate. The gatekeeper immediately closed the door and said, "Remain inside!"

He said, "Why?"

The gatekeeper said, "You are a tricky fellow. All those ten have escaped to the other place, now I cannot allow you to go. At least one journalist should be here."

The journalist said, "But I cannot remain here! You have to let me go!"

The gatekeeper said, "Are you mad? You spread that rumor, which is absolutely false. They got the idea that they will get great jobs in hell, and became excited—but why are you wanting to go?"

He said, "Who knows, there may be something in it. I cannot stay here and miss it. You cannot stop me anyway because I am not supposed to be here; I am only a tourist for twenty-four hours. Remember, that was our basic decision—that for twenty-four hours I will be in, and then I will go out. You cannot stop me—you cannot go against your word."

But the gatekeeper tried hard: "You have spread the rumor; it is absolutely false. And don't bring trouble on me because the hierarchy, the bureaucracy, will ask me, 'Where are all the ten journalists?' Once in a while they take the census and they'll say, 'Not a single journalist? The whole quota is missing? Where have they gone?'

"At least I can show the hierarchy the man who convinced them;

and they escaped. And because it has never happened before—anybody escaping from paradise into hell—we don't keep the doors closed from the inside. Nobody ever escapes; anybody can open them and look out, there is no problem. Who is going to want to go to hell? And there is no third place. So the doors were open as always, and they escaped. They simply said to me, 'Good-bye, we are not coming back again.' I cannot let you go."

But the journalist was stubborn. He said, "Then I will go immediately to the hierarchy and expose the whole thing: that I am not entitled to be here, I don't have a green card—I am just a tourist—and the gatekeeper is not allowing me to go out. You have committed two crimes: first, you allowed me in; second, you are not allowing me out."

The gatekeeper understood; that was perfectly right. He said, "Okay, you go. The census, it takes eternity—everything takes eternity here. Meanwhile maybe some other journalist may turn up. But this is strange, that you are convinced by a rumor that you created yourself."

He said, "When ten other journalists believe it, there must be something in it. Some part of it must be true; otherwise how can you convince ten journalists to go from paradise to hell? There is bound to be some truth in it."

The leader is continuously in need of being convinced again and again that what he is saying is right. For that he needs growing numbers of committed people. And the more fanatically they are committed, the more convincing they are to him. If they are ready to die or to kill, to go on a crusade, do *jihad,* holy war—that makes him certain.

And in a circular way, his certainty convinces the followers—because he becomes louder, more stubborn; he becomes absolutely certain. *Ifs* and *buts* disappear from his language—whatever he says is the *truth*. And this vicious circle goes on and on. It makes the leader fanatic and the followers fanatics. It is the psychological need of both; both are in the same boat.

People have a psychological need to feel certain. To have shifting sand continuously underneath their feet makes their life difficult. It is difficult enough as it is—and then all around, uncertainty and insecurity, all around, problems and no answers. This gives an opportunity to those few cunning people who can pretend that they deal exactly in the commodities you need. The only quality the leader needs is that he should always be ahead of the crowd. He should be constantly watchful of where the crowd is going, and be ahead of it. That keeps the crowd feeling that the leader is leading.

The leader only has to be this clever, that he goes on watching the mood of the people, where they are moving. Wherever the wind starts blowing the real leader never misses the chance: He is always ahead of the crowd.

Thinkers are not needed because a thinker will start wondering whether the way the crowd is going is the right course, or whether the way he was going is the right course. If he starts thinking in that way then he will not be the leader any longer, he will be alone. The crowd will have moved with some idiot who does not bother to wonder about where they are going. You may be going to hell, but he is the leader—he is ahead of you. The only quality in the leader that is needed is a faculty that can judge the mood of the crowd. This is not very difficult because the crowd is shouting loudly what it wants all the time, where it wants to go, what its needs are. You have just to be a little alert and put all these voices together; then there will be no problem, you will be ahead of the crowd.

And go on promising whatever they are asking for—nobody will expect you to fulfill your promises, they are asking only to be promised. Who has asked you to fulfill your promises? Go on giving promises and

> The only quality the leader needs is that he should always be ahead of the crowd. He should be constantly watchful of where the crowd is going, and be ahead of it. That keeps the crowd feeling that the leader is leading.

don't be worried that some day they will catch hold of you and ask about them. They never will, because whenever they catch hold of you, you can give them bigger promises.

And people's memories are very short. What you promised five years ago, who remembers? In five years' time so much water has gone down the Ganges, who bothers? In five years so much has changed. Don't be worried, you just go on making bigger and bigger promises.

> Fanatic commitment to groups and organizations, political, religious, or any other kind, is a kind of addiction—just like any other drug.

And people believe in those promises, people want to believe. They have nothing else, just hopes. So the leaders go on giving opium, hope, and people become addicted.

Fanatic commitment to groups and organizations, political, religious, or any other kind, is a kind of addiction—just like any other drug. A Christian feels at home surrounded by Christians. That is addiction, a psychological drug. Seeing a person outside of their crowd, something in the psyche of people immediately starts trembling: a question mark has arisen. There is a man who does not believe in Christ: "It is possible not to believe in Christ? It is possible to survive without believing in Christ?" Suspicions, doubts . . .

Why do they get angry? They are not angry, they are really afraid. And to hide the fear they have to project the anger. Anger is always to hide fear.

People use all kinds of strategies. There are people who will laugh just so that they can stop their tears. In laughing you will forget, they will forget . . . and the tears can remain hidden. In anger, their fear remains hidden.

They are very fanatic, defensive . . . They know their belief is not their experience, and they are afraid some outsider may scratch, may dig deep, may bring the wound in front of their eyes. Somehow they have been able to cover it up—they are Christians and Christ is the savior, the only savior, the only real savior, and they have the Holy Book and God is with them so what is there to fear? They have created a cozy psychological home and suddenly, like a bull in a china shop, in comes a stranger who doesn't believe as they do!

One of my teachers loved me very much. In my high school days he was the one teacher with whom I was very intimate. So after I went to university, and came back to my hometown on holidays, I would go to see him.

He said one day, "I wait for you. It is very strange that I wait for you, knowing that now the holidays are here and you will be coming. And your coming is just like a fresh breeze. In my old age you remind me again of my youth and my youthful dreams. But when you come, I become afraid and I start praying to God: 'Let him go as soon as possible!' Because you create suspicion in me; you are my greatest doubt. Just seeing you is enough for all my doubts to start arising. Somehow I keep them down, but with you it is difficult."

He said, "It is strange that just your coming into my house is enough and all my efforts at repression fail and all my doubts stand up. I know that I don't know God, and I know that my prayers are just futile—there is nobody to hear them. Still I go on doing them three times a day: morning, afternoon, evening. But when you are here then I cannot do my prayers as peacefully as I do every other day."

I said, "But I never disturb your prayers!"

He said, "It is not that you disturb them. But if you are just sitting here and I am doing my prayer . . . it is impossible. Suddenly I know that what I am doing is stupid and I know what you are thinking. You must be thinking that this old fool still goes on doing the same thing . . . I know that in your eyes this is not intelligent, what I am doing. And the trouble is, that deep down I agree with you. But now I am too old and I cannot change. Fear arises. I cannot stop. Many times I have thought, Why don't I stop praying? But I have been praying for seventy-five years . . ."

At that time he must have been about ninety-two. "I have been praying for so long. And now, at the time of death, to stop? And who
knows? . . . If this boy is around and God really does exist, then I will be
in a fix: I will not be able even to raise my eyes before God if at the last
moment I dropped praying. So I think, now that I have done it all my
life, let me continue, right or wrong. If it is wrong, nothing is lost. Anyway, now that I am retired, the whole day I am free. And if God is there,
then it is perfectly good—my prayers have succeeded."

I said, "This won't help. Even if God is there, this kind of prayer is
futile. Do you think you can deceive God? Won't he ask you? You were
praying with this idea that if he does not exist, good, and if he exists,
you can say that at least you prayed to him. You think you can deceive
God?"

He said, "This is the trouble. That's why I say to you, please don't
come! I cannot drop it, and I cannot do it sincerely. And now you have
created a third problem: Even if I am doing it, it is useless! Because you
are right: If God is there he will know this simple thing, that this old man
is trying to deceive him."

I said, "This is far worse than not praying. At least be honest. And I
don't think being honest is anything against religion. Just be honest; if
you don't feel it, drop it!"

He said, "With you I again start feeling young, strong. But when you
are gone I am again old, death is close by, and this is not the time to
change boats. One may fall into the water. It is better to keep on with
what you are doing . . . whatever is going to happen, let it happen. Just
continue. And I am not alone; two hundred million Hindus are with me.
That's the point, two hundred million Hindus are with me."

I said, "Yes, that's true. Two hundred million Hindus are with you
and I am alone. But a single person can destroy your two hundred million Hindus' support, if it is based on a lie. You have taken a wrong
step—you should never have listened to me!"

That's what fanaticism is: Don't listen to anything that goes against
you. Before anybody says something you start shouting so loudly that you

hear only your own voice. Read only your own book, listen only to your church, to your temple, to your synagogue.

Fanaticism is simply a strategy to protect you from doubts. But although doubts can be protected, they cannot be destroyed. And now there is no need either. Man has passed through those stages where he needed crowds. Now he can be an individual. That does not mean that you don't have clubs, you don't have societies, but there is no need to be committed fanatically.

You can be a Rotarian; that does not mean you are committed fanatically, that you will die for the Rotary Club. That will be a really great martyrdom— somebody dying for the Rotary Club! You don't have to die for the Rotary Club, Lions' Club . . . you need not die for Christianity, Mohammedanism, Hinduism, communism, socialism. You can have a rapport with people, you can have a dialogue with people. You can have meetings with people, you can commune with people who are of the same mind, but there is no need to make any fuss about it. No crusade, no holy war . . .

Yes, you can remain a nation but there is no need to make too much of those boundaries that you have created on the map. They are only on the map, don't start seeing them on the ground. That's where you become blind.

It is perfectly good there should be so many nations but there is no need for so many madnesses. It is perfectly good, people can worship in their own ways, pray in their own ways, have their own book, love their own messiahs, there is no problem about it. But don't

> You can remain a nation but there is no need to make too much of those boundaries that you have created on the map. They are only on the map, don't start seeing them on the ground. That's where you become blind.

make it a problem for other human beings. It is your personal thing. You like something, you prefer a certain perfume—perfectly good; if somebody else does not like it, it does not make him your enemy. These are preferences—somebody can differ. And differing does not mean antagonism, it simply means one has a different way of looking at things, feeling things.

There is no need for any fanaticism, there is no need for any commitment. If we can have organizations in the world without commitment, without fanaticism, it will be a beautiful world. Organizations themselves are not bad. Organizations without commitment, without fanatic attitudes, simply make an orderly world. And order is certainly needed. Where there are so many millions of people you cannot live without order.

I have called that order a "commune." I have called it "commune" just to make it different from organization, political party, religious cult. I have called it simply "commune," where people of similar vision live in a friendliness, with all their differences.

They are not to erase their differences to be part of the commune, that becomes commitment. Their differences are accepted, those are the qualities of those individuals.

And it is in fact making the commune rich when so many people with so many different qualities, talents, creativities, sensitivities, are joined without crippling each other, without destroying each other. On the contrary, they are helping each other to become a perfect individual, a unique individual . . .

STEPPING OUT OF THE PYRAMID

A question: I was shocked to hear you say that the pyramid of humanity consists of Ayatollah Khomeini and Albert Einstein, and there is no qualitative difference between the two. Isn't there a third alternative?

I am shocked too, but one is helpless against the reality. The truth is that there is no qualitative difference between Ayatollah Khomeini and Albert Einstein; I would have loved to declare it if there was even a small possibility of some qualitative difference. That does not mean that both are the same type of person.

Ayatollah Khomeini is a madman. Albert Einstein is a genius, the sharpest intelligence humanity has ever produced. So I am not saying that they are the same kind of people, but what can I do? They belong to the same range. The Ayatollah is the lowest in the line, Albert Einstein the highest, but the difference is only of degrees; it is the same pyramid.

Ayatollah Khomeini, Adolf Hitler, Joseph Stalin, Benito Mussolini, Mao Tse-tung—they are as human as Albert Einstein, Bertrand Russell, Jean-Paul Sartre, Karl Jaspers; they belong to one humanity, to one mind. But Ayatollah Khomeini and his company are sick. The mind is the same but it is a sick mind, it is upside down. Albert Einstein and Bertrand Russell are healthy. It is the same mind but in the right shape; it is as it should be.

But I cannot say that they belong to two different categories; that would be a lie. It would be consoling—you would not be shocked, I would not be shocked, everybody would be happy. But to destroy truth for such stupid consolation is not going to help anybody.

But why do you look only from one side? There are many aspects which have to be considered. Why don't you see it as a great revelation? You have thought only of one thing, that's why you got shocked. I got shocked too, but I also got excited, ecstatic.

You thought only of one thing, that Albert Einstein is reduced to the level of Ayatollah Khomeini. But why can't you see the other possibility— that Ayatollah Khomeini can be raised to the level of Albert Einstein?

I am opening a tremendous possibility for these mad people. And these mad people have dominated humanity; something has to be done. Humanity as such is not bad, not evil, but one Ayatollah Khomeini can drive a whole country crazy, idiotic.

The names, the words, the principles these people use to hide their madness and stupidity are beautiful. Ayatollah Khomeini recites the holy Koran every day. He does not need to read; he has memorized it—the whole holy Koran. He quotes continuously from the holy Koran, and those who are listening to him and following him believe that he is a prophet, a messenger of God sent to help Islam succeed. That's what all the religions believe: If they succeed, only then is there any future for humanity; otherwise there is no future, man is finished. And what he is doing is so barbarous, so ugly, so inhuman . . . People are being slaughtered continuously, beheaded continuously. People are being beaten to death on the crossroads before thousands of spectators—and all those spectators are rejoicing because this is the success of Islam.

Ayatollah Khomeini says that anything done according to the Islamic principles is right. There is no other way, no other criterion to decide right and wrong. To behead a man is Islamic. If the man is not willing to become a Mohammedan then it is better he should die. Living as a non-Mohammedan is worse than dying, because death may change his life pattern. Perhaps in this body, in this mind, he is incapable of becoming a Mohammedan, so this body and mind have to be destroyed. These are hindrances to his salvation. And to die by the hands of Islamic soldiers is a glory in itself. You should be proud: You attained a great death. You could not attain a great life but you attained a great death. So the person who is being killed by the Islamic murderers is fortunate. And the people who are killing him are also earning great virtue, because there is no other motive—they are trying to help the man, to transform his being. They are making the way to God clear and clean for the person. They are doing God's work: They will be born as saints in paradise. So both are benefited. How can something be wrong and evil when both parties are immensely benefited, spiritually benefited?

Do you see the cunningness of people? But this Ayatollah has the same mind as you have, it is just that it has gone nuts. But it can be repaired.

This is happening all over the world . . . Just the other day in the Vatican one woman jumped from St. Peter's basilica—the highest church in Christendom—and killed herself. Nobody knows why, and perhaps nobody will ever know why. But when I heard this, the immediate response that came to me was that this woman has declared something significant. The whole of humanity is going to die in the Vatican, jumping from St. Peter's basilica. This woman is a pioneer. She has simply said that this is going to happen to the whole of humanity. And they are doing everything—the pope, the cardinals, the bishops, the priests—to encourage this to happen.

A very respected humanitarian, a Catholic nun, Sister Judith Vaughan, was expelled from the Catholic church. In California she was running a shelter for poor women, abandoned women, rejected women. And she helped thousands of women. But all her life's work is nothing; she just committed a small mistake, a mistake in the eyes of the Christian bureaucracy. She signed a newspaper advertisement in favor of abortion rights. The newspaper had asked those who were in favor to sign and send the advertisement back to the newspaper, so they could say that not all Christians are against the right to abortion. Sister Judith signed it—and that is a great sin.

The woman worked her whole life, served thousands of women, was respected all over California, and she understands the problems of women—abortion, children, orphans—more than those idiots who expelled her from the church. Not only did they expel her from the church, they prevented her from entering the shelter that she created for poor women, for suffering women. She was not allowed to enter the church or the shelter, and she is no longer a nun. Nobody cares that what she was doing was humanitarian.

More population means more problems—and you are not able to solve the problems that are present. Each child brings thousands of problems with him. Already more people have arrived on the earth than the earth can support. Even countries like America have problems which should have disappeared from the world long before—what to say about the third world, the poor world? Africa, Latin America, Asia—what to say of those countries?

In America there are millions and millions of illiterate adults. In the richest country of the world—technologically, scientifically, culturally, in every way at the top—millions of adults are still uneducated, they can't read a newspaper. And you go on bringing more people? You cannot even solve simple problems—and there are complicated problems.

In a gas explosion in Bhopal thousands of people died. All the women that were pregnant and did not die then started giving birth to children. Thousands of children were coming out of the womb dead or crippled or blind or retarded. A few which were born alive died within six weeks. The physicians and the scientists did not think that the gas was going to affect the fetus so severely. And this was only a small explosion. When your nuclear explosions and atomic explosions start happening, how they are going to affect you is unimaginable. And it will not affect only you; it will affect all the generations that follow you. It will affect the whole future of humanity.

Who is creating these problems? The mind. The same mind can solve them.

So when I say Ayatollah Khomeini and Albert Einstein belong to the same line . . . if you think that Albert Einstein is also like Ayatollah Khomeini you will get only a shock. But if you also think that Ayatollah Khomeini has the capacity to be an Albert Einstein then you will be excited like me.

But I have talked only about the pyramid of the mind. I have not talked about people who have dropped out of the mind, I have not talked about the meditators. They are qualitatively different from both.

A man of meditation is as far away from Ayatollah Khomeini as he is from Albert Einstein, because he is far away from mind itself.

The pyramid is only of people living in the mind, so don't be depressed. You can jump out of the pyramid; nobody is forcing you to be in it. It is your decision to be in it or not to be in it. You can become a watcher. You stand outside the pyramid and watch the whole stupid game that goes on.

I am not part of the pyramid. That's why I can talk about the pyramid, describe it in total detail from all aspects, because I am just a watcher. I can move around the pyramid, I can see all its faces. I can see its lowest depth, I can see its highest peak—because I am not in it.

If you are in it, then it is impossible for you to watch it in its totality; you have to be outside of it. And there have been such people down the ages—very few, but that does not make any difference: Even if a single person can escape from the pyramid that is enough to prove the possibility. And many have escaped from it.

Just a little effort on your side, a little alertness, and you can slip out of the mind—because the pyramid is not made of something solid; the bricks it is made out of are thoughts. You are surrounded by a wall of thoughts. It is so easy to come out of it. You don't even have to dig a hole in the wall, you don't even have to open a door. You have simply to stand silently and see whether the wall really exists or only appears to.

In the East they call it a mirage; it only appears real. The closer you come to it, and the better you look at it, the more it starts disappearing. Thoughts are the most insubstantial things in the world; they don't have anything material in them.

Your thoughts are just like ghosts. You simply go on believing in them, never trying to have an encounter, never turning yourself toward them and staring at them. You will be simply surprised that any thought that you stare at simply melts away. It cannot stand your watchfulness.

So there is a third alternative. You need not be either Ayatollah

> You are surrounded by a wall of thoughts. It is so easy to come out of it. You don't even have to dig a hole in the wall, you don't even have to open a door. You have simply to stand silently and see whether the wall really exists or only appears to.

Khomeiniac or Albert Einstein. Albert Einstein is a good man, but good and bad are two sides of the same coin. Saint and sinner are two sides of the same coin; heaven and hell, God and devil—two sides of the same coin. Neither can exist without the other.

But there is a third alternative—you need not be either—and that's really to be yourself.

To be out of the pyramid of the mind is to enter into the temple of your being.

The pyramid is for the dead. Actually the pyramids were made as graves for Egyptian kings and queens. They are graveyards; and when I used the word *pyramid* for the mind I used it knowingly. Mind is also a graveyard of dead things, past memories, experiences, shadows . . . all shadows. But by and by they become so thick that they create a dark curtain around you.

If you want to escape from your shadow, what do you think you have to do? Run? The shadow will follow you wherever you go, it will be with you; it is your shadow. And a shadow is nonexistential; it is a ghost. The only way to get rid of it is to turn back and look at it and try to find whether there is any substance in it. There is nothing! It is pure negativity. It is just because you are standing in the way of the sun rays that the sun rays cannot come in; and the absence of sun creates the shadow.

Exactly this is the situation about your thoughts. Because you are not watchful, because you are not silent, because you can't see things clearly without any disturbance, thoughts are substitutes for awareness. Unless you become aware, thoughts will continue.

The mind is not you; it is somebody else: You are only a watcher. And just a few glimpses of watching will prepare you to get out of the pyramid without any fighting, without any struggle, without any practice. You simply stand up and get out.

People go on believing in anything that is consolatory. Their ghosts, their gods, their heaven and hell—these are all just consolations. Their saints, holy men, sages—all consolation. A true man needs guts to get out of all this rotten mess. And the only way to get out of it is to become a witness of your own thought processes. And it is easy, it is the easiest thing in the world. You just have to do it once; but you never try even once, and you go on thinking it is the most difficult thing.

I also used to think that it was a very difficult thing, because that's what I had been told by everybody, read in every book—that it is such a great, difficult phenomenon; it takes lives together for a man to come to the state of no-mind. When everybody is saying that, and there is not even a single exception, it is very natural that you may start believing it.

But I am a little eccentric. My logic does not follow the ordinary course, it goes zigzag. Once I became aware that everybody says it is difficult, every scripture says it is difficult, the first idea that came to me was that it is possible that nobody has tried. Otherwise there would be different opinions. Somebody would say it is this difficult; somebody would say it is more difficult than that; somebody would say it is less difficult than that. It is impossible to have unanimous support for its difficulty from all over the world. The only possibility was that nobody had tried—but nobody wants to confess one's ignorance. Then the best course is to agree with the collective consensus that it is difficult, very difficult; it takes lives.

I dropped that idea. I said, "It has to happen in this life; otherwise I will not let it happen in any life, I will struggle against it. Either this life or never." "Now or never" became my fixed approach, and the day I decided "Now or never," it happened. Since then I have been simply amazed how people have been fooled.

The simplest thing has been made the most impossible—and the simplest thing opens the door for the third alternative.

It takes you out of the pyramid: You are no longer a mind. And then only do you know who you are. And to know it is to have achieved everything worth achieving.

FROM MIND TO NO-MIND

When somebody becomes identified with the intellect, intellectuality is born; when somebody remains the master, unidentified with the intellect, intelligence is born. Intellect is the same. The whole thing depends on whether you get identified with it or you remain transcendental to it. If you become identified, it is intellectuality; if you remain unidentified, it is intelligence.

Intelligence is of tremendous importance; intellectuality is a barrier. Intellectuality is a barrier even in the world of science. Intellectuality can, at the most, give you scholars, wordy people who go on and on, spinning and weaving systems of thought with no substance at all.

In the scientific endeavor, intelligence has to be focused on the objective world; in the spiritual exploration, intelligence has to move inward. It is the same intelligence, only the direction changes. In science, the object, the outer object, is the goal of inquiry; in the spiritual realm your subjectivity, your interiority, is your adventure. The intelligence is the same.

If you become an intellectual then you will not be a scientist. You will write histories of science or philosophies of science, but you will not be a scientist, an explorer, an inventor, a discoverer on your own. You will be simply accumulating information. Yes, that too has a certain use; as far as the outside world is concerned, even information has a certain limited utility. But in the inner world it has no utility at all. It is a barrier; it has a negative effect on the inner experience.

The intellect is neither a barrier nor a bridge—intellect is neutral. Get identified with it, it becomes a barrier; remain unidentified with it, it is a bridge. And without meditation you cannot know your transcendental nature.

In science, concentration is enough; at the most, contemplation is needed. In the inner world, meditation is the only way. Concentration is not needed—it is not a help, it is a positive hindrance. Contemplation also is not a help; it is a compensation for not being meditative, it is a poor substitute for it. Meditation—only meditation—can bring the inner revolution.

Meditation means getting out of the mind, looking at the mind from the outside. That's exactly the meaning of the word *ecstasy*: to stand outside. To stand outside of the mind makes you ecstatic, brings bliss to you. And great intelligence is released. When you are identified with the mind you cannot be very intelligent because you become identified with an instrument, you become confined by the instrument and its limitations. And you are unlimited—you are consciousness.

> Use the mind, but don't become it. Use it as you use other machines. Mind is a beautiful machine. If you can use it, it will serve you; if you cannot use it and it starts using you, it is destructive, it is dangerous.

Use the mind, but don't become it. Use it as you use other machines. Mind is a beautiful machine. If you can use it, it will serve you; if you cannot use it and it starts using you, it is destructive, it is dangerous. It is bound to take you into some trouble, into some calamity, into some suffering and misery, because a machine is a blind thing. It has no eyes, it has no insight.

Mind cannot see; it can only go on repeating that which has been fed into it. It is like a computer; first you have to feed it. That's what your so-called education is, you go on feeding it. Then it becomes a great storehouse of memory in you, so whenever you need to remember anything it can supply it. But you should remain the master so that you can use it; otherwise it starts directing you.

Don't be guided by your car; remain a driver. You have to decide the direction, you have to decide the goal. You have to decide about the speed, when to start and when to stop. When you lose control and when the car takes over and it starts going on its own you are doomed.

> Information is good if it is stored in the memory and whenever you need it you can find it easily. It is dangerous only when you don't need it and it goes on throwing itself at you.

I am not absolutely against information. Information is good if it is stored in the memory and whenever you need it you can find it easily. It is dangerous only when you don't need it and it goes on throwing itself at you. When it forces you to do something, when you are just a victim, then it is dangerous. Otherwise it is beautiful. It is a beautiful means, but it is not the end.

At Bible school the teacher was asking his class questions. He turned to Jenkins: "Who knocked down the walls of Jericho?"

"Please, sir," replied Jenkins. "It was not me."

The teacher was very annoyed. He went to the headmaster and said, "I have just asked Jenkins who knocked down the walls of Jericho and he said it was not him. What do you think about that?"

The headmaster said, "I have known the Jenkins family for years, and if he said it wasn't him, it wasn't."

Now the teacher was even more annoyed. He phoned the Minister of Education and said, "I asked a boy in class, 'Who knocked down the walls of Jericho,' and he said it wasn't him. I then went to the headmaster to complain about the boy. He said he had known the family for years and if the boy said it wasn't him, it *wasn't* him. What do you think about that?"

The minister was silent for a second, then said, "Listen, I am fed up with complaints from your school. Get the walls repaired, and if there are more complaints I am going to shut that school down!"

Information is not bad in itself—you have to know who knocked down the walls of Jericho! But if information becomes so powerful in your mind that it goes on and on and you cannot switch it off, you cannot put the mind in a state of relaxation, then the mind becomes weary, tired, bored, exhausted. In that state, how can you be intelligent? Your energies are dissipated. Intelligence needs overflowing energies. Intelligence needs health, wholeness.

A meditator will be more intelligent than anybody else. And a meditator will be able to use his mind objectively and subjectively both. He will be able to move inside as easily as he is able to move outside. He will be more flexible. He is the master. He can take the car forward, he can take the car backward.

When Ford made his first car there was no reverse gear in it. It was a difficult problem to come back home. You had to go round, you had to take the long route, just to come back home. Even if you had gone a few yards past your garage, you could not back up to the garage—there was no reverse gear. Later on it was added.

Meditation gives you a reverse gear. Ordinarily you don't have it, and you have to go round the world again and again and still you cannot find where your home is. You cannot come back, you cannot go in; you know only how to go out. A meditator becomes more fluid, more flexible. His life becomes richer.

I am not in favor of those people who in the past, in the name of religion, became fixated in their introversion; that is another extreme. A few people are fixated as extroverts—as a reaction, a few other people become fixated as introverts. Both become dead. Life belongs to the flexible, to one who can move from extroversion to introversion and from introversion to extroversion as easily as you move outside and inside your house. When it is too cold inside you come out in the sun; when it becomes too hot you come inside under the shelter, into the coolness of the house, and there is no problem. It is as simple as that.

Meditation does not mean going against the outside world. It has been so in the past. That's why religion has failed, it could not succeed; it could not have succeeded in any way. Life belongs to the fluid, to the flowing. Whenever you become fixated you become a thing.

> Life belongs to the flexible, to one who can move from extroversion to introversion and from introversion to extroversion as easily as you move outside and inside your house.

Your monks were introverts; they closed their eyes to the outside world. That's why in the East we could not develop science, although the first steps of science were taken in the East. Mathematics was developed in India. The first steps toward technology were taken in China. But there it stopped for the simple reason that the greatest people in the East became fixed as introverts; they lost interest in the objective world, they closed themselves totally to the objective. This is being only half of your total potential.

The West has done just the opposite: It has become utterly extroverted, it does not know how to go in. It does not believe that there is any "in," it does not believe in any soul. It believes in man's behavior, not in man's inner existence. It studies the behavior of man and it says it is all mechanical, there is nobody inside it. Man has become a robot. If you don't know the soul, man becomes a robot. He is understood to be just a beautiful mechanism developed over millions of years—the long, long journey of evolution—but he is only a sophisticated machine.

It was not difficult for Adolf Hitler to kill so many people so easily for the simple reason that if man is a machine, what is the harm in killing people? If you destroy your wristwatch you don't feel guilty; however sophisticated it was, it was only a wristwatch. If you decided to destroy it, it is for you to decide; nobody can object. You cannot be dragged into court as a murderer.

Stalin could kill millions of people easily without any prick in his conscience for the simple reason that Marxism believes that there is no soul. Man is nothing but matter; consciousness is only a by-product of matter. This is one extreme.

Science developed in the West, but spirituality disappeared. In the East, spirituality developed but science disappeared. In both ways man remains poor, and living only half his potential. My effort is to create the whole human being, who will be able to be scientific and spiritual together.

A big, mangy dog was threatening a mother cat and her kittens. He had backed them into the corner of a barn, when suddenly the cat reared back on her hind legs and started barking and growling loudly. Startled and confused, the dog turned and ran from the barn, its tail tucked between its legs.

Turning to her kittens, the mother cat lifted a paw and told them, "Now do you see the advantage of being bilingual?"

I want human beings to be bilingual. They should know science as much, as deeply, as they should know meditation. They should know mind as much as they should know meditation. They should know the language of the objective world—that is science—and they should know also the language of the subjective world—that is spirituality.

Only a person who is able to bridge the objective and the subjective, a person who is able to bridge the East and the West, a person who is able to bridge the materialist and the spiritualist, can be a whole person. The world is waiting for the whole human being. If the whole human being does not arrive soon, then there is no future for humanity. And the whole human being can come only through deep, profound intelligence.

I am not against intellect, I am not against intelligence; I am against intellectuality. Don't get identified with your mind. Always remain a watcher on the hills—a witness to the body, to the mind, a witness to the outer and to the inner, so that you can transcend both the outer and the inner and you can know that you are neither—you are beyond both.

FROM THINKING TO UNDERSTANDING

Thinking is the absence of understanding. You think because you don't understand. When understanding arises, thinking disappears. It is like a blind man groping his way; when you have eyes, you don't grope for the way, you see it. Understanding is like having eyes; you see, you don't grope. Thinking is groping—not knowing what is what, you go on thinking, guessing.

> You think because you don't understand. When understanding arises, thinking disappears.

Thinking cannot give you the right answer because thinking can only repeat that which is known. Thinking has no vision for the unknown. Have you ever tried thinking about the unknown? How will you think about it? You can think only about that which you already know; it is repetitive. You can go on thinking it again and again, you can make new combinations of old thoughts, but nothing really is new.

Understanding is fresh, new. It has nothing to do with the past. Understanding is here, now. It is an insight into reality.

With thinking there are questions and questions and no answers. Even sometimes when you feel that you have found an answer, it is just because one has to decide in some way or other. It is not really the answer, but you have to decide in order to act, so some answer has to be clung to. And if you look deeply into your answer, you will see a thousand and one questions arising out of it.

Understanding has no questions but only answers, because it has eyes.

Thinking is borrowed. All your thoughts are given by others to you. Watch—can you find a single thought that is yours, authentically yours, that you have given birth to? They are all borrowed. The sources may be known or unknown, but they are all borrowed. The mind functions like a computer, but before the computer can give you any answer you have to feed it. You have to supply all the information; then it will give you the answer. That's what the mind has been doing.

Mind is a biocomputer. You go on collecting data, knowledge, information, and then when a certain question arises your mind supplies the answer out of that collection. It is not a real response; it is just out of the dead past.

What is understanding? Understanding is pure intelligence. That pure intelligence is originally yours; you are born with it. Nobody can give you intelligence. Knowledge can be given to you, not intelligence. Intelligence is your own sharpened being. Through deep meditation one sharpens one's being; through meditation one drops borrowed thoughts,

> Watch—can you find a single thought that is yours, authentically yours, that you have given birth to? They are all borrowed. The sources may be known or unknown, but they are all borrowed.

77

reclaims one's own being, reclaims one's originality—reclaims one's childhood, innocence, freshness. Out of that freshness, when you act, you act out of understanding. And then the response is total, here-now; and the response is because of the challenge, not because of the past.

> Knowledge can be given to you, not intelligence. Intelligence is your own sharpened being.

For example, somebody asks you a question—what do you do? You immediately go inside the mind and find the answer. You immediately go into the basement of the mind where you have collected all your knowledge, and find the answer there. Then it is thinking.

Somebody asks a question and you become silent; you look into the question with penetrating eyes; not into the memory, but into the question. You face the question, you encounter the question. If you don't know, you say you don't know. For example, somebody asks whether God exists or not. You immediately say, "Yes, God exists." From where is this answer coming? From your memory? Your Christian memory, Hindu memory, Muslim memory? Then it is almost useless, futile. If you have a communist memory you will say, "No, there is no God." If you have a Catholic memory you will say, "Yes, there is a God." If you have a Buddhist memory you will say, "There is no God." But these answers are coming from the memory. If you are a person of understanding you will simply listen to the question, you will go deep into the question. You will simply watch. If you don't know, you will say, "I don't know." If you know, only then will you say you know. And when I say "if you know," I mean, if you have realized.

A man of understanding is true. Even if he says, "I don't know," his ignorance is more valuable than the knowledge of the mind, because at least his ignorance, his acceptance of the ignorance, is closer to truth. At least he is not trying to pretend, he is not a hypocrite.

Watch, and you will see that all your answers come from your memory. Then try to find the place where memory does not function and pure consciousness functions. That is what understanding is.

I have heard . . .

The doctor stepped into the patient's room. Five minutes later he came out and asked for a corkscrew, then he went back to his patient. In another five minutes he was out again and demanded a chisel and hammer.

The distraught husband couldn't stand it any longer. He pleaded, "For heaven's sake, Doctor, what is wrong with my wife?"

"I don't know yet," the doctor replied. "I can't get my bag opened."

Sometimes even when you say, "I don't know," it is not necessarily coming out of understanding. It may be simply that you can't open your bag. It may be that you cannot open your memories, or you are not able to find something in the memory; you need time. You say, "I don't know. Give me time, let me think about it." What will you do by thinking? If you know, you know; if you don't know, you don't know. What are you going to think about? But you say, "Give me time, I will think about it." What are you saying? You are saying, "I will have to go into the basement of my mind and search. And there is such rubbish accumulated through the years that it is difficult to find, but I will do my best."

Meditate, and become free from this basement. It is not that the basement is not useful; it can be used. But it should not become a substitute for your understanding.

A man of understanding looks into things directly. His insight is direct. But he can use all his accumulation of knowledge to help the insight to reach you. He can use all that he has accumulated to make everything that he is trying to convey to you clear. But that which he is trying to convey is his own. The words may be borrowed, language may be borrowed—has to be borrowed—concepts may be borrowed, but not what he is trying to convey to you. The container will come from the memory, but the contents will be his insight.

And of course, one who has no understanding is continuously a victim of so many thoughts, because he has no one insight to give him a center. He has a crowd of thoughts, unrelated to each other, even diametrically opposite to each other—contradicting each other, with deep antagonism toward each other. He has a crowd—not even a group, not even a society, but a mob—of thoughts buzzing inside the mind. So if you go on with your thinking too far, one day you will become mad. Too much thought can create insanity.

In primitive societies, madness is rare. The more civilized a society is, the more people go insane. Even in civilized societies, more people go insane who work with their intellects. This is unfortunate but this is a fact: More psychoanalysts go mad than in any other profession. Why? Too much thinking. It is very difficult to manage so many contradictory thoughts together. In trying to manage them, your whole being becomes a chaos.

Understanding is single, understanding is central. It is simple; thoughts are very complex.

A henpecked husband visited a psychiatrist and said he had a recurring nightmare.

"Every night," he said, "I dream I am shipwrecked with twelve beautiful women."

"What's so terrible about that?" asked the psychiatrist.

"Have you ever tried cooing for twelve women?"

That was his problem: how to coo for twelve women. Even to coo for one woman is difficult.

Thinking is like cooing for thousands and thousands of women around you. One naturally goes mad. Understanding is very simple: You are married to one insight, but that insight works like a light, a torch. Wherever you focus your torch, mysteries are revealed. Wherever you focus your torch, darkness disappears.

Try to find your hidden understanding. And the way is to drop thinking. And to drop thinking there are two possibilities: either meditation or love.

FROM REACTION TO RESPONSE

Reaction is from the thoughts and response is understanding. Reaction comes from the past; response is always in the present. But ordinarily we react—we have everything already ready inside. Somebody is doing something and we react as if a button has been pushed. Somebody insults you and you become angry—that has happened before, and it has been happening the same way all the while. It has become almost like a button: Somebody pushes it, you become angry. There is not a single moment of waiting, not a single moment where you look at the situation to see if it may be different. The person who is insulting you may be right. He may have simply revealed a truth to you and that's why you feel insulted. Or he may be absolutely wrong, or he may be just a nasty person. But you have to look into the person—if he is right, you have to thank him because he has shown something to you. He has shown compassion toward you, he has been friendly by bringing a truth to your heart. Maybe it hurts, but that is not his fault.

Or maybe he is simply stupid, ignorant. Not knowing anything about you, he has blurted out something. Then there is no need to be angry; he is simply wrong. Nobody is worried about something that is absolutely wrong. Unless it has some truth in it, you are never irritated by it. You can laugh at it, at the whole absurdity of it. It is ridiculous.

Or the person is just nasty and that is his way. He is insulting to everybody. So he is not doing anything to you in particular; he is simply being himself—that's all. So in fact, nothing needs to be done. He is just that type of person.

Somebody insulted Buddha. His disciple Ananda said, "I was getting very angry and you kept quiet. You should have at least allowed me to say something; I would have put him right."

Buddha said, "You surprise me. First he surprised me, and now you surprise me. Whatever he was saying is simply irrelevant. It is unconnected with us, so why get into it? But you surprise me even more: You have become very annoyed, you look angry. This is foolish. To punish oneself for somebody else's error is foolish. You are punishing yourself. Cool down. There is no need to be angry—because anger is fire. Why are you burning your own soul? If he has committed some mistake, why do you punish yourself? It is stupid." But we react.

I have heard . . .
One man was saying to one of his friends, "To please my wife, I have given up smoking, drinking, and playing cards."
"That must make her very happy," said his friend.
"No, it has not. Now, every time she begins to talk to me, she can't think of anything to say."

People live mechanical, robotlike lives. If your wife has been continuously nagging you to stop smoking, and you think she will be happy if you stop, you are wrong. If you smoke she is unhappy, and if you stop smoking she will be unhappy because then she will not find any excuse to nag you.

One woman said to me that she didn't want her husband to be perfect. I asked, "Why?" She said, "Because I love nagging." If the husband is perfect what are you going to do? You will be simply at a loss.

Watch yourself, watch others, and see how they are behaving in a mechanical way—unconscious, like somnambulists, sleepwalkers.

Reaction is of the mind; response is of the no-mind.

FROM BELIEF TO FAITH

Belief is of the mind, of the thinking; faith is of no-mind, of awareness, understanding.

> It happened in a hillside village: the hunter said to his guide, "This seems to be a very dangerous cliff. It's a wonder they don't put up a warning sign."
>
> "They had one up for two years," the native guide admitted, "but no one fell off the cliff so they took it down."

Belief is blind—you believe because you have been taught to believe, but it never goes very deep because it has no understanding of the situation. It is just a superfluous tag, just something added to you. It has not grown from you, it has not been a growth of your understanding. It is just borrowed, so it never penetrates your being. For a few days you carry it, and then seeing that it is useless and nothing is happening, you put it aside. There are Christians who are not Christians; there are Hindus who are not Hindus. They are Hindus only because of those beliefs that they have never used, those beliefs that they have never respected. They think they are Christians, Hindus, Mohammedans, but how can you be a Mohammedan if you have not lived your belief?

But the truth is that belief *cannot* be lived. If one starts becoming more alert, watching life, responding, then by and by a faith arises. Faith is yours; belief is somebody else's. Drop beliefs so that faith can arise. And don't be satisfied with beliefs, otherwise faith will never arise.

FROM SYMPATHY TO COMPASSION

Sympathy is of the mind: You feel somebody is in trouble, somebody is in misery; you think somebody is in misery and you have to help. You have been taught to help, to be of service, to be dutiful, to be a good human being, to be a good citizen, to be this and that. You have been taught, so you feel sympathy.

Compassion has nothing to do with your teachings. Compassion arises as an empathy, not as a sympathy. Compassion arises when you can see the other person as he is, and when you can see him so totally that you start feeling him. You start feeling in the same situation.

It happened: Ramakrishna was moving from one bank to another of the Ganges, near Dakshineshwar. On the other shore, a few people had surrounded a fisherman and they were beating him. Ramakrishna was in the middle of the river. He started crying and weeping, and he started shouting, "Stop, don't beat me!" The people who were sitting around him, in the boat, his disciples, could not believe what was happening: "Who is beating you?" they said. "What are you saying, have you gone mad?" He said, "Look! They are beating me there on the other side."

Then they looked; they saw that the people were beating the man. And Ramakrishna said, "Look at my back." He uncovered his back—there were marks on his back, he was bleeding. It was impossible to believe. The disciples rushed to the other shore, caught hold of the man who was beaten and uncovered his back: He had exactly the same marks.

This is empathy—putting oneself into somebody else's place so totally that what is happening to him starts happening to you. Then compassion arises. But these states are all of no-mind.

FROM COMMUNICATION TO COMMUNION

Communication is of the mind—verbal, intellectual, conceptual. Communion is of no-mind, of deep silence; a transfer of energy, nonverbal; a jump from one heart to another—immediate, without any medium.

The basic, most essential thing to remember—because it divides your life, it divides the whole world into two worlds—is that if you are looking through a screen of thoughts, then you live in one world. The world of thoughts is the world of belief, thinking, sympathy. If you are looking with clean eyes, unclouded eyes, your perception has a clarity. It is pure, just seeing into things as they are, not projecting anything upon them. Then you have understanding, then you have meditation. Then the whole world changes. And the problem is that mind can deceive you. It creates sympathy. It creates false coins: In place of compassion it creates sympathy. Sympathy is a false coin. In place of communion it has only communication, which is a false coin. Instead of faith it has belief, which is a false coin.

Remember it—the mind tries to substitute. Are you lacking something? The mind tries to substitute for it. Be very alert, because whatever the mind can do is going to be false. Mind is the great falsifier, the greatest deceiver there is. It helps, it tries to console you, it gives you something false so that you no longer hanker for the real.

For example, if during the day you have fasted, in the night you will dream of food, dining in great restaurants, or being invited to the palaces of the kings and eating beautiful food. Why? The whole day you have been hungry, now it is difficult to sleep because of the hunger; the mind creates a substitute, a dream. Have you not watched it? In the night your bladder is full and you would like to go to the bathroom, but if you do your sleep will be disturbed—the mind immediately creates a dream that you are in the bathroom. Then you can go on sleeping. It gives you a substitute. The substitute is a consolation. It is not real, but for the time being it helps.

So beware of mind's consolations. Seek reality, because only reality can fulfill you. Consolations can never be fulfilling.

> Beware of the mind's consolations. Seek reality, because only reality can fulfill you. Consolations can never be fulfilling.

You can eat as much food as you like in your dreams, you can enjoy the fragrance of it, the taste of it, the color of it, everything—but it is not going to be nourishing. Belief can give you the whole fragrance of faith, the taste, the color. You can enjoy it but it will not nourish you. Only faith can nourish.

Always remember: That which nourishes you is real, and that which simply gives you a consolation is very dangerous. Because of this consolation you will not seek the real food. If you start living in dreams and you don't eat real food, then by and by you will dissipate, disappear, become dry, and you will be dead.

So take immediate action: Whenever the mind is trying to give you a substitute, don't listen to it. It is a great salesman, a great seducer. It convinces you, it says, "These things are cheap. Faith is very difficult to find because you will have to risk your life; belief is easy, very cheap. You can get it for nothing." In fact, so many people are ready—if you accept their belief they are ready to give you something more with it: Become a Christian, become a Hindu, become a Mohammedan. People are ready to give you a great welcome and respect, respectability. Everything is available; just accept their belief. Belief is not only cheap, it can even bring many more things with it.

Faith is dangerous, never cheap. Understanding is dangerous, never cheap. The real is dangerous. You will have to put your whole life at stake. It needs courage.

THE MASTER AND THE SERVANT

I have heard an ancient story:

A king was very happy with one of his servants. He was so devoted, so totally devoted to the king; he was always ready to sacrifice his life for the king. The king was immensely happy, and many times he had saved the king, risking his own life. He was the king's bodyguard.

One day the king was feeling so happy with the man, he said, "If you desire anything, if you have any desire, just tell me and I will fulfill it. You have done so much for me that I can never show my gratitude, I can never repay you, but today I would like to fulfill any of your wishes, whatsoever it is."

The servant said, "You have already given me too much. I am so blessed just by being always with you—I don't need anything."

But the king insisted. The more the servant said, "There is no need," the more the king insisted. Finally the servant said, "Then it's okay. You make me the king for twenty-four hours and you be the guard."

The king was a little apprehensive, afraid, but he was a man of his word and he had to fulfill the desire. So for twenty-four hours he became the guard and the guard became the king. And do you know what the guard did? The first thing that he did, he ordered the king to be killed, sentenced to death!

The king said, "What are you doing?"

He said, "You keep quiet! You are simply the guard and nothing more. It is my wish and now I am the king!"

The king was killed, and the servant became the king forever.

Servants have their own devious ways to become masters.

The mind is one of the most beautiful, the most complex, the most evolved mechanisms. It has served you well, it continues to serve you well. Because of its services you have repeated the same story in your life—everybody has repeated the same story. You have made the mind the master, and now the master treats you just like a servant.

This is the problem—not that the mind has to be thrown out. If you throw the mind out you will go insane. Without the mind there is only one profession you can be in, and that is politics!

I have heard that a man—it must be some story from the future—a man went to the hospital because his brain was damaged in a car accident and he wanted a new one. So he asked the surgeon to show him all the kinds of brains available. The surgeon took him around; there were many brains. The first brain belonged to a professor, a mathematician. He asked the price—fifty dollars. He was surprised: a famous mathematician, a Nobel laureate, just fifty dollars! Then there was a musician, and his was only thirty dollars. Then there was a businessman's brain and it was only twenty dollars. And so on, so forth. Finally they came to the brain of a politician—it was five thousand dollars! The man was puzzled. He said, "Why does it cost so much?" The surgeon said, "Because it has never been used."

You will need all the mind you have— just be the master of it. Use it, and don't be used by it.

And that's what meditation is all about: the art of moving away from the mind, being above the mind, becoming transcendental to the mind, knowing that "I am not the mind." That does not mean that you have to throw out the mind. Knowing that you are not the mind makes you again the master. Then you can use the mind. Right now, the mind is not within your hands.

> The mind is one of the most beautiful, complex, evolved mechanisms. It has served you well, it continues to serve you well. But because of its services you have made the mind your master, and now it treats you just like a servant.

KNOWN, UNKNOWN, UNKNOWABLE

Intelligence is the clear insight into things about which you don't have any information. Memory can function only with those things which are known to you—but life consists of the known, of the unknown, and of the unknowable. As far as the known is concerned, memory is enough.

That's what all your universities and all your educational systems are doing: They are simply feeding your memory with more and more information, and whatever is known to your memory system, you will be able to answer immediately. That answer does not prove that you are intelligent.

Intelligence is known only when you encounter the unknown, about which you don't have any memory, any knowledge, any information beforehand. When you encounter the unknown, that is the point which is decisive. How do you respond?

Intelligence means the capability to respond to new situations. It comes from your being—the mind is only a vehicle—a kind of awareness of what the mind is, without belonging to it. Intelligence is the quality of the witness; it watches the mind and it gives direction to the mind.

> When you encounter the unknown, that is the point which is decisive. How do you respond? Intelligence means the capability to respond to new situations. It comes from your being—the mind is only a vehicle.

A story:

The student Doko came to the master and asked, "In what state of mind should I seek the truth?"

The master replied, "There is no mind, so you cannot put it in any state, and there is no truth, so you cannot seek it."

Doko said, "If there is no mind and no truth, why do all these students gather before you every day to study?"

The master looked around and said, "I don't see anyone."

The inquirer asked, "Then who are you teaching?"

"I have no tongue, so how can I teach?" replied the master.

Then Doko said sadly, "I cannot follow you; I cannot understand."

The master said, "I don't understand myself."

Life is such a mystery, no one can understand it, and one who claims that he understands it is simply ignorant. He is not aware of what he is saying, of what nonsense he is talking. If you are wise, this will be the first realization: Life cannot be understood. Understanding is impossible. Only this much can be understood—that understanding is impossible. That is what this beautiful Zen anecdote says.

The master says, "I don't understand it myself." If you go and ask the enlightened ones this will be their answer. But if you go and ask the un-enlightened ones they will give you many answers, they will propose many doctrines; they will try to solve the mystery which cannot be solved. It is not a riddle. A riddle can be solved, a mystery is unsolvable by its very nature—there is no way to solve it. Socrates said, "When I was young, I thought I knew much. When I became old, ripe in wisdom, I came to understand that I knew nothing."

It is reported of one of the Sufi masters, Junnaid, that he was working with a new young man. The young man was not aware of Junnaid's inner wisdom, and Junnaid lived such an ordinary life that it needed very penetrating eyes to realize that you were near a buddha. He worked like an ordinary laborer, and only those who had eyes would recognize him. To recognize Buddha was very easy—he was sitting under a Bodhi tree; to recognize Junnaid was very difficult—he was working like a laborer, not sitting under a Bodhi tree. He was in every way absolutely ordinary.

One young man was working with him, and that young man was continually showing his knowledge, so whatsoever Junnaid would do, he would say, "This is wrong. This can be done in this way, it will be better." He knew about everything. Finally Junnaid laughed and said, "Young man, I am not young enough to know so much."

This is really something. He said, "I am not young enough to know so much." Only a young man can be so foolish, so inexperienced. Socrates was right when he said, "When I was young, I knew too much. When I became ripened, experienced, I came to realize only one thing— that I was absolutely ignorant."

Life is a mystery; that means it cannot be solved. And when all efforts to solve it prove futile, the mystery dawns upon you. Then the doors are open; then you are invited. As a knower, nobody enters the divine; as a child, ignorant, not knowing at all, the mystery embraces you. With a knowing mind you are clever, not innocent. Innocence is the door.

This Zen master was right when he said, "I don't understand it myself." It was very deep, really deep, the deepest answer possible. But this is the last part of the anecdote. Start from the very beginning . . .

The disciple came to the Zen master and said, "In what state of mind should I seek the truth?" The master said, "There is no mind so there cannot be any state of mind."

Mind is the illusion, that which is not but appears to be, and appears to be so much that you think that you *are* the mind. Mind is *maya*, mind is just a dream, mind is just a projection . . . a soap bubble floating on a river. The sun is just rising, the rays penetrate the bubble; a rainbow is created and nothing is there in it. When you touch the bubble it is broken and everything disappears—the rainbow, the beauty—nothing is left. Only emptiness becomes one with the infinite emptiness. Just a wall was there, a bubble wall. Your mind is just a bubble wall—inside, your emptiness; outside, my emptiness. It is just a bubble, prick it, and the mind disappears.

The master said, "There is no mind, so what type of state are you asking about?" It is difficult to understand. People come to me and they say, "We would like to attain a silent state of mind." They think that the mind can be silent; mind can never be silent. Mind means the turmoil, the illness, the disease; mind means the tense, the anguished state. The mind cannot be silent. When there is silence there is no mind. When silence comes, mind disappears; when mind is there, silence is no more. So there cannot be any silent mind, just as there cannot be any healthy disease. Is it possible

> The mind cannot be silent. When there is silence there is no mind. When silence comes, mind disappears; when mind is there, silence is no more.

to have a healthy disease? When health is there, disease disappears. Silence is the inner health; mind is the inner disease, inner disturbance.

So there cannot be any silent mind, and this disciple is asking, "What type, what sort, what state of mind should I achieve?" Point-blank, the master said, "There is no mind, so you cannot achieve any state." So please drop this illusion; don't try to achieve any state in the illusion. It's as if you are thinking to travel on the rainbow and you ask me, "What steps should we take to travel on the rainbow?" I say, "There is no rainbow. The rainbow is just an appearance, so no steps can be taken." A rainbow simply appears; it is not there. It is not a reality, it is a false interpretation of the reality.

The mind is not your reality; it is a false interpretation. You are not the mind, you have never been a mind, you can never be the mind. That is your problem—you have become identified with something which is not. You are like a beggar who believes that he has a kingdom. He is so worried about the kingdom—how to manage it, how to govern it, how to prevent anarchy. There is no kingdom, but he is worried.

Chuang Tzu once dreamt that he had become a butterfly. In the morning he was very much depressed. His friends asked, "What has happened? We have never seen you so depressed." Chuang Tzu said, "I am in a puzzle, I am at a loss, I cannot understand. In the night, while asleep, I dreamt that I had become a butterfly."

So the friends laughed. "Nobody is ever disturbed by dreams. When you awake, the dream has disappeared, so why are you disturbed?"

Chuang Tzu said, "That is not the point. Now I am puzzled: If Chuang Tzu can become a butterfly in the dream, it is possible that now the butterfly has gone to sleep and is dreaming that she is Chuang Tzu." If Chuang Tzu can become a butterfly in the dream, why not the other? The butterfly can dream and become Chuang Tzu. So what is real— whether Chuang Tzu dreamt that he has become a butterfly, or the butterfly is dreaming that she has become Chuang Tzu? What is real? Rainbows are there. You can become a butterfly in the dream. And you have become a mind in this bigger dream you call life. When you awaken you don't achieve an awakened state of mind, you achieve a no-state of mind, you achieve no-mind.

What does no-mind mean? It is difficult to follow. But sometimes, unknowingly, you have achieved it. You may not have recognized it. Sometimes, just sitting ordinarily, not doing anything, there is no thought in the mind—because mind is just the process of thinking. It is not a substance, it is just a procession. You are here in this auditorium where I am speaking. I can say a crowd is here, but is there really something like a crowd? Is a crowd substantial, or are only individuals here? By and by individuals will go away, then will there be any crowd left behind? When individuals have gone, there is no crowd.

The mind is just like a crowd; thoughts are the individuals. And because thoughts are there continuously, you think the process is substantial. Drop each individual thought and finally nothing is left.

There is no mind as such, only thinking.

The thoughts are moving so fast that between two thoughts you cannot see the interval. But the interval is always there. That interval is you. In that interval there is neither Chuang Tzu nor the butterfly—because the butterfly is a sort of mind and Chuang Tzu is also a sort of mind. A butterfly is a different combination of thoughts, Chuang Tzu again a different combination, but both are minds. When the mind is not there, who are you—Chuang Tzu or a butterfly? Neither. And what is the state? Are you in an enlightened state of mind? If you think you are in an enlightened state of mind this is again a thought, and when *thought* is there *you* are not. If you feel

> There is no mind as such, only thinking. The thoughts are moving so fast that between two thoughts you cannot see the interval. But the interval is always there. That interval is you.

that you are a buddha, this is a thought. The mind has entered; now the process of thinking is there, again the sky is clouded, the blueness lost. You can no longer see the infinite blueness.

Between two thoughts, try to be alert—look into the interval, the space in between. You will see no mind; *that* is your nature. Because thoughts come and go—they are accidental—but that inner space always remains. Clouds gather and go, disappear—they are accidental—but the sky remains. You are the sky.

Once it happened that a seeker came to Bayazid, a Sufi mystic, and asked, "Master, I am a very angry person. Anger happens to me very easily; I become really mad and I do things. I cannot even believe later on that I can do such things; I am not in my senses. So, how to drop this anger, how to overcome it, how to control it?"

Bayazid took the head of the disciple in his hands and looked into his eyes. The disciple became a little uneasy, and Bayazid said, "Where is that anger? I would like to see into it."

The disciple laughed uneasily and said, "Right now, I am not angry. Sometimes it happens." So Bayazid said, "That which happens sometimes cannot be your nature. It is an accident. It comes and goes. It is like clouds—so why be worried about the clouds? Think of the sky which is always there."

This is the definition of consciousness, *atma,* the Self—the sky which is always there. All that comes and goes is irrelevant; don't be bothered by it, it is just smoke. The sky that remains eternally there never changes, never becomes different. Between two thoughts, drop into it; between two thoughts it is always there. Look into it and suddenly you will realize that you are in no-mind.

The master was right when he said, "There is no mind, so there cannot be any state of mind. What nonsense are you talking?"

But the nonsense has its own logic. If you think that you have a mind, you will start thinking in terms of "states"—an ignorant state of mind, an enlightened state of mind. Once you accept mind, once you accept the illusory, you are bound to go on dividing it. And once you accept that the mind exists, you will start seeking something or other.

The mind can exist only if you keep seeking something. Why? Seeking is desire, seeking is moving into the future, seeking creates dreams. So somebody is seeking power, politics, somebody is seeking riches, kingdoms, and then somebody is seeking the truth. But seeking is there, and *seeking* is the problem, not *what* you are seeking. The object is never the problem, any object will do. The mind can hang on to any object. Any excuse is enough for it to exist.

The master said, "There is no state of mind because there is no mind. And there is no truth, so what are you talking about? There can be no seeking."

This is one of the greatest messages ever delivered. It is very difficult; the disciple cannot conceive that there is no truth. What does this master mean when he says that there is no truth? Does he mean that there is no truth?

No, he is saying that for you, who are a seeker, there can be no truth. Seeking always leads into the untrue. Only a nonseeking mind realizes that which is. Whenever you seek, you have missed that which is. Seeking always moves into the future, seeking cannot be here and now. How can you seek here and now? Here and now, you can only *be*. Seeking is desire—future enters, time comes in—and this moment, this here and now is missed. Truth is here, now.

If you go to a buddha and ask, "Is there God?" he will deny it immediately: "There is no God." If he says there is, he creates a seeker; if he says there is God, you will start seeking. How can you remain quiet when there is God to be sought? Where should you run to find him? You have created another illusion.

For millions of lives you have been a seeker, after this or after that, this object, that object, this world or that world, but a seeker. Now you are a seeker after truth but the master says there is no truth. He cuts away the very ground of seeking, he pulls away the very ground where you are standing, where your mind is standing. He simply pushes you into the abyss.

The inquirer said, "Then why are these many seekers all around you? If there is nothing to seek and no truth, then why this crowd?" The inquirer went on missing the point. The master looked around and said, "I don't see anyone, there is no one here." The inquirer went on missing the point because the intellect always goes on missing. He could have looked. This was the fact: There was no one.

If you are not seeking you are *not,* because it is seeking that gives you the ego. Right this moment, if you are not seeking anyone, anything, then you are not here—there is no crowd. If I am not teaching anything—because there is nothing to be taught, no truth to be taught—if I am not teaching anything and if you are not learning anything, who is here? Emptiness exists, and the bliss of pure emptiness. Individuals disappear and it becomes an oceanic consciousness.

Individuals are there because of individual minds. You have a different desire, that's why you differ from your neighbor. Desires create distinctions. I am seeking something, you are seeking something else; my path differs from yours, my goal differs from yours. That's why I differ from you. If I am not seeking and you are not seeking, goals disappear, paths are no longer there. How, then, can the minds exist? The cup is broken. My tea flows into you and your tea flows into me. It becomes an oceanic existence.

The master looked around and said, "I don't see anyone—there is no one."

But the intellect goes on missing. The inquirer said, "Then whom are you teaching? If there is no one, then whom are you teaching?" And the master said, "I have got no tongue, so how can I teach?" He goes on giving hints to become alert, to look, but the inquirer is engulfed in his own mind. The master goes on hitting, hammering on his head; he is talking nonsense just to bring him out of his mind.

If you had been there you would have been convinced by the inquirer, not by the master. The inquirer would have appeared to be exactly right. This master seemed to be mad, absurd. He was talking! And he said, "There is no tongue, so how can I talk?"

He was saying, "Look at me, I am without form. Look at me, I am not embodied. The body appears to you but I am not that, so how can I talk?"

The mind goes on missing. This is the misery of the mind. You push it, it again gathers itself; you hit it, and for a moment there is a sinking and a trembling, and again it is established.

Have you seen the Japanese doll? They call it a *daruma* doll. You throw it whatever way—topsy-turvy, upside down—but whatever you do, the doll sits in a buddha posture. The bottom part is so heavy you cannot do anything. Throw it in any way and the doll again sits in a buddha posture. The name *daruma* comes from Bodhidharma; in Japan, Bodhidharma's name is Daruma. Bodhidharma used to say that your mind is just like this doll. He would throw it, kick it, but whatsoever he did he could not disturb the doll; the bottom part was so heavy. You throw it upside down, it will come right side up.

So this master went on pushing. A little shaking, and the doll sat up straight again, missed the point. Finally, desperate, the inquirer said, "I don't follow, I don't understand." And with the ultimate hit, the master said, "I don't understand myself."

I go on teaching, knowing well there is nothing to be taught. That's why I can go on infinitely. If there were something to be taught I would have finished already. Buddhas can go on and on because there is nothing to be taught. It is an endless story, it never concludes, so I can go on and on. I will never be finished; you may be finished before my story ends, because there is no end to it.

Somebody was asking me, "How do you manage to go on talking every day?" I said, "Because there is nothing to be taught." Someday you will suddenly feel it—that I am not talking, that I am not teaching. You have realized there is nothing to be taught because there is no truth.

What discipline am I giving to you? None. A disciplined mind is again a mind, even more stubborn, more adamant; a disciplined mind is more stupid. Go and see the disciplined monks all over the world—Christian, Hindu, Jain. Whenever you see a man who is absolutely disciplined you will find a stupid mind behind it. The flowing has stopped. He is so concerned with finding something that he is ready to do whatever you say. If you say, "Stand on your head for an hour," he is ready to stand on his head. It is because of desire. If God can be achieved only through standing on his head for hours, he is ready, but he must achieve.

I am not giving you any achieving, any desiring; there is nowhere to reach and nothing to achieve. If you realize this, you have achieved this very moment. This very moment you are perfect; nothing is to be done, nothing is to be changed.

That's why the master said, "I don't understand it myself." It is difficult to find a master who says, "I don't understand it myself." A master has to claim that he knows, only then will you follow him. A master must not only claim that he knows, he must claim that *only* he knows, nobody else: "All other masters are wrong, I alone know." Then you will follow. You must be absolutely certain, then you become a follower. The certainty gives you the feeling that here is the man, and if you follow you will reach.

I will tell you one story. It happened once, a so-called master was traveling. In every village he would go, he would declare, "I have achieved, I have known the divine. If you want, come and follow me."

People would say, "There are many responsibilities. Someday, we hope we will be able to follow you." They would touch his feet, give him respect, serve him, but nobody would follow because there were many other things to be done first before one went to seek the divine. First things first. The divine is always the last, and the last thing never comes because the first are infinite; they are never finished. But in one village, a madman— he was mad, otherwise who would follow this master—said, "Right. Have you have found God?"

The master hesitated a little, looking at the madman— because this man seemed dangerous, he might follow and create trouble—but in front of the whole village he couldn't deny it, so he said, "Yes."

The madman said, "Now, initiate me. I will follow you to the very end. I want to realize God myself." The so-called master became perturbed, but what to do? The madman started following him, he became just like his shadow. One year passed. The madman said, "How far, how far is the temple?" He said, "I am not in a hurry but how much time will be needed?" By this time the master had become very uncomfortable and uneasy with this man. This madman would sleep next to him, he would move with him; he had become his shadow. And because of him, his certainty was dissolving. Whenever he would say, in a village, "Follow me," he would become afraid, because this man would look at him and say, "I am following you, master, and still I have not reached."

The second year passed, the third year passed—the sixth year passed, and the madman said, "We have not reached anywhere. We are simply traveling to different villages and you go on telling people, 'Follow me.' I am following—whatsoever you say, I do it, so you cannot say I am not following the discipline."

The madman was really mad—whatever was told to him he would do. So the master couldn't deceive him by saying that he was not trying hard enough. Finally, one night, the master said to him, "Because of you I have lost my own path. Before I met you I was certain; now I am no more. Now you please leave me."

Whenever there is someone certain and you are mad enough, you start following. Can you follow this type of man who says, "I myself don't know. I myself don't understand?" If you can follow this man, you will reach. You have already reached if you decide to follow this man, because it is the mind that asks for certainty, the mind that asks for knowledge. The mind also asks for dogmatic assertions, so if you can be ready to follow a man who says, "I don't know myself," seeking has stopped. Now you are not asking for knowledge.

One who is asking for knowledge cannot ask for being. Knowledge is rubbish; being is life. When you stop asking for knowledge you have stopped asking about the truth, because truth is the goal of knowledge. If you don't inquire what is, but you become silent, mindless—that which is, is revealed.

Everything is available, has been available always; you have never missed it. But just because of your seeking—because of the future, the goal—you cannot look. The truth surrounds you, you exist in it. Just like the fish exist in the ocean, you exist in the truth. Godliness is not a goal, godliness is what is here and now. These trees, these winds blowing, these clouds moving, the sky, you, I—this is what godliness is. It is not a goal.

Drop the mind *and* the god. God is not an object, it is a merger. The mind resists a merger, the mind is against surrender; the mind is very cunning and calculating.

This story is beautiful. You are the inquirer. You have come to acquire knowledge, to solve the mystery, and I repeat to you: There is no state of mind, because there is no mind. There is no truth, so no seeking makes any sense. All seeking is futile; search as such is foolish. Seek and you will lose. Don't seek and it is there. Run and you will miss. Stop—it has always been there.

And don't try to understand—*be*.

Become ignorant, become like a child. Only the heart of a child can knock at the doors of the beyond, and only the heart of a child is heard.

OUTSIDE THE BOX—
BREAKING FREE OF
CONDITIONING

All kinds of conditionings are poisons. To think of oneself as a Hindu is to think of oneself as opposed to humanity. To think of oneself as German, as Chinese, is to think of oneself as opposed to humanity, is to think in terms of enmity, not friendship.

Think of yourself only as a human being. If you have any intelligence, think of yourself only as a simple human being. And when your intelligence grows a little more you will drop even the adjective *human;* you will think of yourself only as a being. And the being includes all—the trees and the mountains and the rivers and the stars and the birds and the animals.

Become bigger, become huge. Why are you living in tunnels? Why are you creeping into small dark black holes? But you think you are living in great ideological systems. You are not living in great ideological systems, because there are no great ideological systems. No idea is great enough to contain a human being; being-hood cannot be contained by any concept. All concepts cripple and paralyze.

Don't be a Catholic and don't be a communist, just be a human being. These are all poisons, these are all prejudices. And down the ages you have been hypnotized into these prejudices. They have become part of your blood, your bones, your very marrow. You will have to be very alert to get rid of all this poisoning.

Your body is not poisoned as much as your mind is. The body is a simple phenomenon, it can be easily cleaned. If you have been eating nonvegetarian foods it can be stopped, it is not such a big deal. And if you stop eating meat, within three months your body will be completely free of all the poisons created by nonvegetarian foods. It is simple. Physiology is not very complicated.

> Don't be a Catholic and don't be a communist, just be a human being. These are all poisons, these are all prejudices. And down the ages you have been hypnotized into these prejudices.

But the problem arises with psychology. A Jaina monk never eats any poisoned food, never eats anything nonvegetarian. But his mind is polluted and poisoned by Jainism as nobody else's is.

The real freedom is freedom from any ideology. Can't you simply live without any ideology? Is an ideology needed? Why is an ideology needed so much? It is needed because it helps you to remain stupid, it is needed because it helps you to remain unintelligent. It is needed because it supplies you ready-made answers and you need not find them on your own.

The real man of intelligence will not cling to any ideology—for what? He will not carry a load of ready-made answers. He knows that he has enough intelligence so that whatever situation arises, he will be able to respond to it. Why carry an unnecessary load from the past? What is the point of carrying it?

And in fact the more you carry from the past, the less you will be able to respond to the present, because the present is not a repetition of the past, it is always new—always, always new. It is never the old; it may sometimes appear like the old, but it is not old, there are basic differences.

Life never repeats itself. It is always fresh, always new, always growing, always exploring, always moving into new adventures. Your old ready-made answers are not going to help you. In fact they will hinder you; they will not allow you to see the new situation. The situation will be new, and the answer will be old.

That's why you look so stupid in life. But to remain stupid seems cheaper. To be intelligent needs effort, to be intelligent means you have to grow. And growth is painful. To be intelligent means you have to be continuously alert and aware; you cannot fall asleep, you cannot live like a somnambulist.

And to be intelligent has a few more dangers, too. To be intelligent is very difficult because you have to live with the stupid crowds. To live with blind people and have eyes is a dangerous situation; they are bound to destroy your eyes. They cannot tolerate you, you are an offense.

Hence Jesus is crucified, Socrates is poisoned, Al-Hillaj is killed, Sarmad is beheaded. These were the most intelligent people that have ever walked on the earth, and how have we behaved with them? Why did a man of the intelligence of Socrates have to be killed? He became intolerable. His presence became such an offense. To look into his eyes meant to look in the mirror. And we are so ugly that rather than accepting the fact that we are ugly, the easier course is to destroy the mirror and forget all about your ugliness, and start living again in the old dream that you are the most beautiful person in the world.

> The real man of intelligence will not cling to any ideology—for what? He will not carry a load of ready-made answers. He knows that he has enough intelligence so that whatever situation arises, he will be able to respond to it.

We destroyed Socrates because he was a mirror. Hence people have decided it is better to remain mediocre, it is better to remain unintelligent.

Just the other day, I was reading a report. A few psychologists in England have discovered that by the time great politicians reach the highest posts, their intelligence is already withering away. Just think of a man of eighty-four becoming a prime minister! Those psychologists have warned the whole world that this is dangerous. People who have gone beyond the age of sixty, seventy, eighty, they become prime ministers and presidents. This is dangerous for the world because they have so much power and so little intelligence left.

But those psychologists are not aware of another thing that I would like to tell you. In fact those people are chosen to be prime ministers and presidents because they are no longer intelligent. People don't like intelligent persons. People like people who look like them, who are like them; they feel they are not strangers. Intelligent people will be strangers.

> It is certainly dangerous to have unintelligent people in powerful posts. And it is becoming more and more dangerous, because they have more and more power and less and less intelligence. But why does it happen?

I can't think of any country that could choose Socrates to be the prime minister—impossible. He is so different, his approach to life is so different, his insight into things is so deep. No country could afford it, or no country could be so courageous as to make him the prime minister because he would bring chaos. He would start changing each and every thing, because each and every thing needs to be changed.

This rotten society has to be destroyed completely; only then can a new society be created. Renovation is not going to help. We have been renovating the same old ruins for centuries. No more props, no more renovations, no more whitewash! All that is needed is to demolish it, and let us create a new society.

Let us bring a new human being, *Homo Novus.* Let us give birth to something new, a new mind, a new consciousness.

People choose dull, dead persons to be in power because you can be safe with them. Countries choose mediocre people to be in power because they will save their tradition, their conventions, their prejudices. They will protect their poisons. Instead of destroying them, they will enhance them and strengthen them.

It is certainly dangerous to have unintelligent people in powerful posts. And it is becoming more and more dangerous, because they have more and more power and less and less intelligence. But why does it happen? There is a subtle logic in it. People don't want to change. Change is arduous, change is difficult.

A DIFFERENT KIND OF DISOBEDIENCE

It is important to understand what I mean by *disobedience.* It is not the disobedience you will find in the dictionaries. My idea of disobedience is not to hate being told what to do or to do just the opposite of what you are told, in reaction.

Obedience needs no intelligence. All machines are obedient; nobody has ever heard of a disobedient machine. Obedience is simple, too. It takes from you the burden of any responsibility. There is no need to react, you have simply to do what is being said. The responsibility rests with the source from where the order comes. In a certain way you are very free: You cannot be condemned for your act.

After the Second World War, in the Nuremberg trials, so many of Adolf Hitler's top men simply said that they were not responsible, and they didn't feel guilty. They were simply being obedient—whatever they were told to do, they did it, and they did it with as much efficiency as they were capable of. In fact to make them responsible and condemn them, punish them, to send them to the gallows, according to me, was not fair. It was not justice, it was revenge. If Adolf Hitler had won the war, then Churchill's people, Roosevelt's people, Stalin's people, or they them-selves would have been in the same situation and they would have said exactly the same—that they were not responsible.

If Stalin had been on the stand in court, he would have said that it was the order of the high command of the communist party. It was not his responsibility because it was not his decision; he had not done any-thing on his own. So if you want to punish somebody, punish the source of the order. But you are punishing a person who simply ful-filled what all the religions teach, and all the leaders of the world teach—obedience.

Obedience has a simplicity; disobedience needs a little higher order of intelligence. Any idiot can be obedient—in fact, only idiots can be obedient. The person of intelligence is bound to ask why: "Why am I supposed to do it? Unless I know the reasons and the consequences of it, I am not going to be involved in it." Then he is being responsible.

Responsibility is not a game. It is one of the most authentic ways of living—dangerous, too—but it does not mean disobedience for disobedi-ence's sake. That will be again idiotic.

There is a story about a Sufi mystic, Mulla Nasruddin. From the very beginning it was thought that he was upside down. His parents were in trouble. If they would say, "Go to the right," he would go to the left. Finally his old father thought that rather than bothering with him, it would be better, if they wanted him to go to the left, to order him to go to the right—he was bound to go to the left.

One day they were crossing the river. They were carrying a big bag of sugar strapped to the donkey and the bag was leaning to the right, so there was a danger that it might slip into the river. It had to remain balanced on the donkey. But to tell Nas-ruddin to move the bag toward the left would mean losing the sugar—he would move it toward the right.

So the father said to Nasruddin, "My son, your bag is slipping; move it toward the right." And Nasruddin moved it toward the right.

The father said, "This is strange, for the first time you have been obedient!"

Nasruddin said, "For the first time you have been cunning. I knew you wanted this to be moved to the left; I could see with my eyes where it needed to be moved. Even in such a subtle way you cannot make me obedient."

But just to go against obedience is not moving your intelligence higher. You remain on the same plane. Obedient or disobedient, but there is no change of intelligence.

To me, disobedience is a great revolution. It does not mean saying an absolute no in every situation. It simply means deciding whether to do it or not, whether it is beneficial to do it or not. It is taking the responsibility on yourself. It is not a question of hating the person or hating to be told, because in that hating you cannot act obediently or disobediently; you act very unconsciously. You cannot act intelligently.

When you are told to do something, you are given an opportunity to respond. Perhaps what is being asked of you is right—then do it, and be grateful to the person who told you at the right moment to do it. Perhaps it is not right—then make it clear. Bring up your reasons, why it is not right. Then help the person to see that what he is asking is going in a wrong direction. But hate has no place. If it is right, do it lovingly. If it is not right, then even more love is needed, because you will have to tell the person, explain to the person, that it is not right.

The way of disobedience is not stagnant, just going against every order and feeling anger and hate and revenge toward the person. The way of disobedience is a way of great intelligence.

So it is not ultimately about obedience or disobedience. Reduced to the basic fact, it is simply a question of intelligence—behave intelligently.

Sometimes you will have to obey, and sometimes you will have to say, "I am sorry, I cannot do it." But there is no question of hate, there is no question of revenge, anger. If hate, anger, or revenge arises, that simply means you know that what is being told to you is right, but it goes against your ego to obey it; it hurts your ego. That hurt feeling comes up as hate, as anger.

But the issue is not your ego; the issue is the action that you have to take—and you have to bring forth your total intelligence to figure it out. If it is right, then be obedient; if it is wrong, be disobedient. But there is no conflict, there are no hurt feelings.

If you are obeying, it is easier; you need not explain to anybody. But if you are not obeying, then you owe an explanation. And perhaps your explanation is not right. Then you have to move back, you have to do it.

A person should live intelligently—that's all. Then whatever he does is his responsibility.

It happens that even great intellectuals are not living intelligently. Martin Heidegger, one of the greatest intellectuals of this age, was a follower of Adolf Hitler. And after Adolf Hitler's defeat and the exposure of his basic animality, brutality, murderousness, violence, even Martin Heidegger shrank back and said, "I was simply following the leader of the nation."

But a philosopher has no business following the leader of the nation. In fact, a philosopher's basic duty is to guide the leaders of the nation, not to be guided by them. Because he is outside of active politics, his vision should be clearer than theirs. He is standing aloof, he can see things that people who are involved in the action cannot see.

But it is easy to throw responsibility on somebody else . . .

If Adolf Hitler had been victorious, I am certain Martin Heidegger would have said, "He is victorious because he followed my philosophy." And certainly Heidegger was a great intellectual compared to Adolf Hitler. Adolf Hitler was just a retarded person. But power . . .

We have been brought up to follow the powerful—the father, the mother, the teacher, the priest, the God. Essentially we have been told that whoever has the power is right: "Might is right, and you have to follow it." It is simple because it needs no intelligence. It is simple because you can never be held responsible, you can never be told that whatever happened was your responsibility.

In all the armies around the world only one thing is taught through years of training, and that is obedience. In Germany, in the Second World War, there were good people—but they were heads of concentration camps! They were good fathers, good husbands, good friends. Nobody could have conceived of it, watching them with their families, with their friends, in the club, that these people were murdering thousands of Jews every day. And they were not feeling guilty at all, because it was only an order from above. That was their whole training, that you have to follow the order. It had become part of their blood and their bones and their marrow: When the order comes, obedience is the only way.

> Obedience is one of the greatest crimes, because all other crimes are born out of it. It deprives you of intelligence, it deprives you of decisiveness, it deprives you of responsibility. It destroys you as an individual.

This is how mankind has lived up to now, and that's why I say obedience is one of the greatest crimes, because all other crimes are born out of it. It deprives you of intelligence, it deprives you of decisiveness, it deprives you of responsibility. It destroys you as an individual. It converts you into a robot.

Hence I am all for disobedience. But disobedience is not just *against* obedience. Disobedience is *above* obedience *and* the so-called disobedience described in the dictionaries. Disobedience is simply the assertion of your intelligence: "I take the responsibility, and I will do everything that feels right to my heart, to my being. I will not do anything that goes against my intelligence."

My whole life, from my childhood to the university, I was condemned for being disobedient. And I insisted, "I am not disobedient. I am simply trying to figure out, with my own intelligence, what is right, what should be done. And I take the whole responsibility for it. If something goes wrong, it was my fault. I don't want to condemn somebody else because he has told me to do it." But it was difficult for my parents, for my teachers, professors.

In my school it was compulsory to wear caps, and I entered the high school without a cap. Immediately the teacher said, "Are you aware or not that the cap is compulsory?"

I said, "A thing like a cap cannot be compulsory. How can it be compulsory to put something on your head? The head is compulsory, but not the cap. And I have come with the head; perhaps you have come only with the cap."

He said, "You look a strange type. It is just written in the school code that without a cap, no student can enter the school."

I said, "Then that code has to be changed. It is written by human beings, not by God; and human beings commit mistakes."

The teacher could not believe it. He said, "What is the matter with you? Why can't you just wear a cap?"

I said, "The trouble is not with the cap; I want to find out why it is compulsory, its reason, its results. If you are unable to explain it, you can take me to the principal and we can discuss it." He had to take me to the principal.

In India, Bengalis are the most intelligent people; they don't wear caps. And Punjabis are the most unintelligent, simple people, and they wear turbans. So I said to the principal, "Looking at the situation—Bengalis don't wear any caps and they are the most intelligent people in the country, and Punjabis wear not only a cap but a very tight turban, and they are the most unintelligent people. If it really has something to do with your intelligence, I would rather not take the risk."

The principal listened to me and he said, "The boy is stubborn, but what he is saying makes sense. I had never thought about it—this is true.

And we can make this code noncompulsory. Anybody who wants to wear a cap can wear one; anybody who does not want to, there is no need—because it has nothing to do with learning."

The teacher could not believe it. On the way back he asked me, "What did you do?"

I said, "I have done nothing, I simply explained the situation. I am not angry, I am perfectly willing to wear a cap. If you feel it helps intelligence, why only one? I can wear two caps, three caps, caps upon caps, if it helps my intelligence . . . I am not angry. But you have to prove the value of it."

The teacher said to me, I still remember his words, "You will be in trouble your whole life. You will not fit in anywhere."

I said, "That's perfectly okay, but I don't want to be an idiot and fit in everywhere. It is good to be 'unfit' but intelligent. And I have come to the school to learn intelligence, so I can be a misfit intelligently! Please never try again to change me from an individual into a cog in the machine."

And from the next day the caps disappeared; only the teacher had come with a cap. And looking at the class and around the school . . . because the new rule had come into force that caps were not compulsory, and all the other teachers, even the principal, had come without caps. He looked so silly. I said to him, "There is still time. You can take it off and put it in your pocket." And he did!

He said, "That's right. If everybody is against the cap . . . I was simply being obedient to the law."

So remember, when I talk about disobedience I don't mean replacing obedience with disobedience. That will not make you better. I use the word *disobedience* only to make it clear to you that it is up to you, that you have to be the decisive factor in all your actions in life. And that gives tremendous strength, because whatever you do, you do with a certain rational support to it.

Just live intelligently.

If something is told to you, decide whether it is right or wrong. Then you can avoid all guilt feelings. Otherwise, if you don't do it, you feel guilty; if you do it, again you feel guilty. If you do it you feel that you are being subservient, that you are not being assertive, that you are not being yourself. And if you don't do it, then you start feeling guilty again—because perhaps it was the right thing to do, and you are not doing it.

There is no need for all this clumsiness. Just be simple. If something is asked of you, respond intelligently. And whatever your intelligence decides, do it this way or that—but *you* are responsible. Then there is no question of guilt.

If you are not going to do it, explain to the person why you are not going to do it. And explain without any anger, because anger simply shows that you are weak, that you don't really have an intelligent answer. Anger is always a sign of weakness. Just plainly and simply explain the whole thing; perhaps the other person may find that you are right and may be grateful to you. Or perhaps the other person may have better reasons than you; then you will be thankful to the other person because he has raised your consciousness.

Use every opportunity in life for raising your intelligence, your consciousness.

Ordinarily what we are doing is using every opportunity to create a hell for ourselves. Only you suffer, and because of your suffering, you make others suffer. And when so many people are living together, if they all create suffering for each other, it goes on multiplying. That's how the whole world has become a hell.

It can be instantly changed.

Just the basic thing has to be understood, that without intelligence there is no heaven.

THE INTELLIGENCE OF INNOCENCE

A child is pure intelligence because a child is yet uncontaminated. A child is a clean slate, nothing is written on him. A child is absolute emptiness, tabula rasa.

The society will start writing immediately that you are a Christian, Catholic, Hindu, Mohammedan, Communist. The society will immediately start writing the Bhagavadgita, the Koran, the Bible on you. The society cannot wait. The society is very much afraid that if the child's intelligence is left intact, then he will never be a part of any slavery, of any structure of domination. He will neither dominate nor be dominated. He will neither possess nor be possessed. He will be a pure rebellion. His innocence has to be corrupted immediately. His wings have to be cut, he has to be given crutches to lean upon so he never learns how to walk on his own feet, so he remains always in a kind of dependence.

First the children are dependent on the parents, and the parents enjoy it very much. Whenever children are dependent, parents feel very good. Their life starts having some meaning: They know that they are helping some new people to grow up, some beautiful people to grow up. They are not meaningless. They have a vicarious enjoyment of being creative. It is not true creativity, but at least they can say that they are doing something, they are occupied. They can forget their own problems in the anxiety of bringing up the children. And the more the children are dependent on them, the more happy they feel. Although on the surface they go on saying they would like their children to be independent, that is only on the surface. A really independent child hurts the parents. They don't like the independent child because the independent child has no need of them.

That is one of the big problems the older generation is facing today: Children in the modern age are not dependent on them, and because they are not dependent you cannot force things upon them. You cannot tell them what to do and what not to do, you cannot be their masters. The old generation is suffering very much. For the first time in human history the old generation is feeling utterly empty, meaningless, because their whole occupation is gone, and their joy in bringing up children is shattered. In fact they are feeling guilty, afraid that they may be destroying the children. Who knows? What they are doing may not be the right thing.

Parents destroy the intelligence of the children because that is the only way to enslave them; then the teachers, school, college, university do the same. Nobody wants a rebel, and intelligence is rebellion. Nobody wants to be questioned, nobody wants his authority to be questioned, and intelligence is questioning. Intelligence is pure doubt. Yes, one day out of this pure doubt arises trust, but not against doubt; it arises only through doubt.

Trust comes out of doubt as a child comes out of the mother's womb. Doubt is the mother of trust. The real trust comes only through doubt, questioning, inquiring. And the false trust, which we know as belief, comes by killing the doubt, by destroying questioning, by destroying all quest, inquiry, search, by giving people ready-made truths.

> ☙
>
> The real trust comes only through doubt, questioning, inquiring. And the false trust, which we know as belief, comes by killing the doubt, by destroying questioning, by giving people ready-made truths.

The politician is not interested in children's intelligence, because leaders are leaders only because people are stupid. And when people are so stupid, they will find stupid leaders. People are so unintelligent that they will be ready to fall into the trap of anybody who can pretend to lead them.

Children are born with pure intelligence, and we have not yet been able to respect it. Children are the most exploited class in the world, even more than women. After women's liberation sooner or later there is going to be children's liberation; it is far more necessary. Men have enslaved women, and men and women both have enslaved the children. And because the child is very helpless, naturally he has to depend on you. It is very mean of you to exploit the child's helplessness. But hitherto parents have been mean. And I am not saying that deliberately or consciously they have been so, but almost unconsciously, not knowing what they are doing. That's why the world is in such a misery, the world is in such a mess. Unconsciously, unknowingly, every generation goes on destroying the next generation.

This is the first generation which is trying to escape out of the trap and this is the beginning of a totally new history. But children certainly are utterly intelligent. You just watch children, look into their eyes, look at the way they respond.

Little Papo seemed to be enjoying himself thoroughly at the zoo with his father. As they were looking at the lions, however, a troubled look came over the boy's face and his father asked him what the matter was. "I was just wondering, daddy . . . In case a lion breaks loose and eats you, what number bus do I take home?

Just watch children, be more observant.

A teacher asked her class of small children to make a drawing of the Old Testament story they liked best. One small boy depicted a man driving an old car. In the back seat were two passengers, both scantily dressed. "It is a nice picture," said the teacher. "But what story does it tell?"

The young artist seemed surprised at the question. "Well," he exclaimed. "Doesn't it say in the Bible that God drove Adam and Eve out of the Garden of Eden?"

No proof of their intelligence is needed! Just look around—children are everywhere, just watch.

Another story I have heard . . .

In another school the teacher had asked the children the same question: to make some pictures of any story that they liked. This child made an airplane instead of a car. The airplane

had four windows. From one window God the Father was looking out, from the other, the Holy Ghost, from the third, Jesus
Christ. But the teacher was puzzled, and asked, "These three I
can understand, but who is this fourth?"

The child said, "That is Pontius the Pilot!"

But nobody watches children. In fact, everybody thinks they are just
a nuisance. They should not be heard, they should only be seen; that has
been the dictum down the ages. Who cares what they ask? Who cares
what they say? Who listens?

A child came running home panting and breathing hard,
and told his mother, "Listen to what happened! A tiger chased
me from the school up to the house! Somehow I managed; I had
to run so hard!"

The mother said, "Listen, I have told you millions of times
not to exaggerate—millions of times not to exaggerate! And here
you go again! You found a tiger in the street? Where is the tiger?"

He said, "You can look out of the window, he is standing
there."

A small dog!

The mother looked and said, "This is a tiger? You know
perfectly well that this is a dog! You go up and pray to God, and
ask for forgiveness!"

So the child left. After a few minutes he came back. And the
mother said, "You prayed? You asked God?"

He said, "Yes! I said, 'God forgive me! It was totally wrong
of me to think of that little dog as a tiger.' And God said, 'Don't
be worried! When I first saw him, I also thought that he was a
tiger!'"

Children have immense intelligence but down the ages they have not
been allowed to develop it.

We have to create a new kind of education in which nothing is imposed on the children, but where they are helped to strengthen their natural, God-given intelligence. They are not to be stuffed with information which is in fact almost useless. Ninety-eight percent of the information that we go on throwing into children's minds is just stupid, foolish. But because of that load, that baggage, the child will never be free of the burden.

I have been a professor in the university, and I have been a student from primary school to university. My own observation is that ninety-eight percent of the information that we go on throwing on children is utterly futile; it is not needed at all. And not only is it futile, it is harmful, positively harmful.

Children should be helped to be more inventive, not repetitive, which is what our education is based on right now. Our whole educational system is geared to repetition. If a child can repeat better than others, then he is thought to be more intelligent. In fact he only has a better memory, not better intelligence. It almost always happens that the man with a very good memory may not have very good intelligence, and vice versa.

> Children should be helped to be more inventive, not repetitive—which is what our education is based on right now. Our whole educational system is geared to repetition.

Albert Einstein didn't have a very good memory. Newton, Edison, and so many more great inventors were really very forgetful of things.

But our whole educational system is centered on memory, not intelligence. Stuff more and more information in the memory, make the man a machine! Our universities are factories where men are reduced to machines. Twenty-five years are wasted—one-third of your life—in making you a machine! And then it becomes really difficult to unwind you again, to make you a human being again.

That is my work. <u>You come as machines, very uptight, full of memories, information, knowledgeability, absolutely in the head</u>, hung up there. <u>You have lost all contact with your heart and your being.</u> To pull you down toward the heart and then toward the being is really a difficult task. But in a better world this will not be needed. Education should help people to become more and more intelligent, not more and more repetitive. Right now it is repetition: You cram into your head whatsoever nonsense is told to you, and then you regurgitate it in the examination papers—and the better you vomit the better marks you get. There is only one thing that you have to remember: to be exactly repetitive. Don't add anything, don't delete anything, don't be inventive, don't be original.

Originality is killed, repetitiveness praised. And intelligence can grow only in the atmosphere where originality is praised.

Innocence is your very nature. You do not have to become it, you are already it. You are born innocent. Then layers and layers of conditioning are imposed upon your innocence. Your innocence is like a mirror and conditioning is like layers of dust. The mirror has not to be achieved, the mirror is already there—or rather, here. The mirror is not lost, it is only hidden behind the layers of dust.

You don't have to follow a way to reach your nature because you cannot leave your nature, you cannot go anywhere else. Even if you wanted to, it is impossible. That's exactly the definition of nature: Nature means that which cannot be left behind, that which cannot be renounced. But you can forget about it. You cannot lose it but it can be forgotten.

And that's exactly what has happened. The mirror is not lost but forgotten—forgotten because it is not functioning anymore as a mirror. Not that any defect has arisen in it, just layers of dust are covering it. All that is needed is to clean it, to remove those layers of dust.

The process of becoming innocent is not really a process of becoming, it is a process of discovering your being. It is a discovery, not an achievement. You don't attain to something new, you simply attain to that which you have always been. It is a forgotten language.

It happens many times: You see a person on the road, you recognize him, his face seems familiar. Suddenly you remember also that you know his name. You say, "It is just on the tip of my tongue," but still it is not coming to you. What is happening? If it is just on the tip of your tongue, then why can't you say it? You know that you know it, but still you are not able to remember it. And the more you try, the more difficult it becomes, because making an effort makes you more tense, and when you are tense you are farther away from your nature, you are farther away from that which is already there. When you are relaxed you are closer; when you are utterly relaxed, it will surface of its own accord.

So you try hard, but it doesn't come, so you forget all about it. Then lying down in your bath, or just swimming in the pool, you are not even trying to remember that man's name when suddenly it bubbles up. What has happened? You were not trying to remember, and you were relaxed. When you are relaxed you are wide, when you are tense you become narrow—the more tense, the more narrow. The passage between you and that which is inside you becomes so narrow that nothing can pass through it, not even a single name.

All the great scientific discoveries have been made in this very mysterious way—in this very *un*scientific way, so to speak.

Madame Curie was working on a certain mathematical problem for three years continuously and the more she tried, the farther and farther away the solution seemed. She tried every possible way, but nothing was working, nothing was happening. And there was somewhere a deep, tacit feeling that "the solution exists. I am not struggling with something absurd." This tacit feeling continued all the time as an undercurrent; hence she could not drop the effort, either. She was getting tired—three years wasted for a single problem. But deep down within herself somebody was saying, "The solution IS possible. This exercise is not futile. Go on." And she went on stubbornly, she persisted. She dropped all other projects, she forced herself totally into the one problem. But the more she tried, the more impossible it became.

One night it happened, almost as it happened to Gautama the Buddha; of course, the problems were different, but the process was the same. Buddha had struggled for six years to attain enlightenment and he had attained nothing. Then one night he dropped the whole effort, went to sleep, and, by the morning when the last star was setting, he became enlightened.

That night Madame Curie dropped the idea, the whole project—she closed the chapter. "Enough is enough! Three years wasted is too much for one problem." There were other problems which were waiting to be solved. It was finished in her mind, although the tacit understanding was still there just like a constant murmur. But she had followed it long enough, it was time. One has only a limited time; three years is too much for one problem. Deliberately she dropped the idea. As far as she was concerned she closed the whole project. She went to sleep never to be bothered by that problem again.

And in the morning when she got up she was surprised. On a piece of paper on her table, the solution was there, written in her own handwriting. She could not believe her eyes. Who had done it? The servant could not have done it—he knew nothing of mathematics, and if Madame Curie had not been able to do it in three years, how could the servant have done it? And there was nobody else in the house. And the servant had not entered in the night—the doors were locked from inside. She looked closely and the handwriting resembled hers.

Then suddenly she remembered a dream. In the dream she had seen that she had got up, gone to the table, written something . . . Slowly, slowly, the dream became clear. Slowly, slowly, she remembered that she had done it in the night. It was not a dream, she had actually done it. And this was the solution! For three years she had been struggling hard and nothing was happening—and the night she dropped the project, it happened. What happened? She became relaxed.

Once you have dropped the effort you become relaxed, you become restful, you become soft, you become wide, you become open. It was there inside her, it surfaced. Finding the mind no longer tense, it surfaced.

Innocence is there, you have simply forgotten it—you have been made to forget it. Society is cunning. For centuries man has learned that you can survive in this society only if you are cunning; the more cunning you are, the more successful you will be. That's the whole game of politics: Be cunning, be more cunning than others. It is a constant struggle and competition as to who can be more cunning. Whosoever is more cunning is going to succeed, is going to be powerful.

After centuries of cunningness man has learned one thing: that to remain innocent is dangerous, you will not be able to survive. Hence parents try to drive their children out of their innocence. Teachers, schools, colleges, universities exist for the simple work of making you more cunning, more clever. Although they call it intelligence it is not intelligence.

Intelligence is not against innocence, remember. Intelligence is the flavor of innocence, intelligence is the fragrance of innocence. Cunningness is against innocence; and cunningness, cleverness, are not synonymous with intelligence. But to be intelligent needs a tremendous journey inward. No schools can help, no colleges, no universities can help. Parents, priests, the society, they are all extroverted; they cannot help you to go

> Intelligence is not against innocence, remember. Intelligence is the flavor of innocence, intelligence is the fragrance of innocence. Cunningness is against innocence.

inward. And buddhas are very rare, few and far between. Not everybody is fortunate enough to find a buddha. Only a buddha can help you to be an intelligent person, but you cannot find so many buddhas who want to become primary school teachers and high school teachers and university professors; it is impossible.

So there is a substitute for intelligence. Cunningness is a substitute for intelligence—a very poor substitute, remember. And not only is it a poor substitute, it is just the opposite of it, too. The intelligent person is not cunning; certainly intelligent, but his intelligence keeps his innocence intact. He does not sell it for mundane things. The cunning person is ready to sell his soul for small things.

> Cunningness is a substitute for intelligence—a very poor substitute, remember. And not only is it a poor substitute, it is just the opposite of it too.

Judas sold Jesus for only thirty silver coins—just thirty silver coins. And a Jesus can be sold. Judas must have thought that he was being very intelligent, but he was simply cunning. If you don't like the word *cunning* you can call him clever; that is just a good name for the same thing, for the same ugly thing.

The society prepares you to be cunning so that you are capable of competing in this struggle for existence, the struggle to survive. It is a cutthroat competition, everybody is after everybody else's throat. People are ready to do anything to succeed, to be famous, to climb the ladder of success, name and fame. They are ready to use you as stepping-stones. Unless you are also cunning you will be simply used, manipulated. Hence the society trains every child to be cunning, and these layers of cunningness are hiding your innocence.

Innocence has not to be achieved, it is already there. Hence it is not a question of becoming, it is your being. It has only to be discovered—or rediscovered. You have to drop all that you have learned from others, and you will immediately be innocent.

Hence my antagonism toward all knowledge that is borrowed. Don't quote the Bible, don't quote the Gita. Don't behave like parrots. Don't just go on living on borrowed information. Start seeking and searching for your own intelligence.

A negative process is needed; it is to be achieved through *via negativa*. That is the Buddha's way. You have to negate all that has been given to you. You have to say, "This is not mine; hence I have no claim over it. It may be true, it may not be true. Who knows? Others say it is so; unless it becomes my experience I cannot agree or disagree. I will not believe or disbelieve. I will not be a Catholic or a communist, I will not be a Hindu or a Mohammedan. I will simply not follow any ideology." Because, whoever you follow, you will be gathering dust around yourself. Stop following.

[. . .]My work is not to teach you something, but to help you to discover yourself. Just drop all knowledge. It hurts because you have carried that knowledge for so long and you have been bragging so much about that knowledge—your degrees, M.A.s and Ph.D.s and D.Litt.s, and you have been bragging about all those degrees. And suddenly I am saying to you: Drop all that nonsense.

Just be as simple as a child. Just be again a child as you were born, as God sent you into this world. In that mirrorlike state you will be able to reflect that which is. Innocence is the door to knowing. Knowledge is the barrier and innocence is the bridge.

THE GIFT OF BEING ALIVE

You have never been accepted by your parents, teachers, neighbors, society, as you are. Everybody was trying to improve upon you, to make you better. Everybody was pointing at the flaws, at the mistakes, at the errors, at the weaknesses, at the frailties that every human being is prone to.

Nobody emphasized your beauty, nobody emphasized your intelligence, nobody emphasized your grandeur.

Just being alive is such a gift, but nobody ever told you to be thankful to existence. On the contrary, everyone was grumpy, complaining. Naturally, if everything surrounding your life from the very beginning goes on pointing out to you that you are not what you should be, goes on giving you great ideals that you have to follow and you have to become . . . Your *isness* is never praised. What is praised is your future—if you can become someone respectable, powerful, rich, intellectual, in some way famous, not just a nobody.

Constant conditioning against you has created in you the idea, "I am not enough as I am, something is missing. And I have to be somewhere else—not here. This is not the place I am supposed to be, but somewhere higher, more powerful, more dominant, more respected, more well known."

Your head, your mind, has been turned in many ways by many people according to their ideas of how you should be. There was not any bad intention. Your parents loved you, your teachers loved you, your society wants you to be somebody. Their intentions were good, but their understanding was very limited. They forgot that you cannot manage to make a marigold into a rose flower, or vice versa.

All that you can do is help the roses to grow bigger, more colorful, more fragrant. You can give all the elements that are needed to transform the color and the fragrance—the manure that is needed, the right soil, the right watering at the right times—but you cannot make the rosebush produce lotuses. And if you start giving the idea to the rosebush, "You have to produce lotus flowers"—and of course the lotus flowers *are* beautiful and big—you are giving a wrong conditioning. Not only will this bush never be able to produce lotuses; its whole energy will be directed on a wrong path so it will not produce even roses, because from where will it get the energy to produce roses? And when it turns out that there are no lotuses, no roses, of course this poor bush will feel continuously empty, frustrated, barren, unworthy.

This is what is happening to human beings. With all good intentions, people are turning your mind. In a better society, with more understanding people, nobody will try to change you. Everybody will help you to be yourself— and to be oneself is the richest thing in the world. <u>To be oneself gives you all that you need to feel fulfilled, all that can make your life meaningful, significant.</u> Just being yourself and growing according to your nature will bring the fulfillment of your destiny.

This is real richness. This is real power.

If everybody grows to be himself, you will find the whole earth full of powerful people, of tremendous strength, intelligence, understanding, and a fulfillment, a joy that they have come home.

> In a better society, with more understanding people, nobody will try to change you. Everybody will help you to be yourself— and to be oneself is the richest thing in the world.

DISCOVERING THE "OFF" SWITCH

Create a little distance. Watch the mind, how it functions, and create the distance. Watching automatically creates distance. Hence again and again the buddhas insist—watch. Watch day and night. Slowly, you will begin to see that you are consciousness and the mind is just an instrument available to you. Then you can use it when needed and when it is not needed you can switch it off. Right now, you don't know how to switch it off; it is always on. It is like a radio in your room that is always on and you don't know how to turn it off—so you have to sleep with the radio on, and it goes on shouting all kinds of advertisements and playing all kinds of songs that you have heard a thousand times. But you don't know how to turn it off. The whole day you are tired, many times you want to get rid of the noise of the radio, but you cannot because you don't know how to turn it off. It is like sleeping with the lights on because you don't know how to turn them off.

Freud remembers that when electricity came to Vienna for the first time, a friend, a villager, came to visit him. Freud took every care of the visitor, took him to the room where he was going to sleep, left him there, and said good night.

The villager was very puzzled by just one thing—the electricity, the electric bulb. He knew how to put out a lamp, how to blow a candle out, but what to do with this electric bulb? He tried all that he knew: standing on a chair, he blew on it many times but nothing would happen to it. He examined it from every angle; there was no hole in it, there was nothing.

How could he imagine that just on the wall there was a switch? That was impossible for him to imagine, he had never seen electricity. But he was also afraid to go and ask Freud or somebody else, because they would think he was a fool . . . "You can't even put the light out—what kind of man are you?" So, feeling embarrassed, he tried to sleep with the light on. He could not sleep. Many times he stood up again on the chair, tried again. The whole night it continued; sleep wouldn't come because of the light—too much light, such a bright light, he had never seen such a bright light. He had known candles, but the bulb must have sent the light of a hundred candles or more into the room. In the morning he was dead tired.

Freud asked him, "You look very tired. Couldn't you sleep?"

He said, "Now there is no point in hiding it, because I am going to stay three days—this bulb is going to kill me! Even to look at it makes a shiver go up my spine. How to turn it off?"

Freud said, "You fool! Why didn't you ask me?"

He said, "I was just feeling embarrassed—so foolish to ask such a simple thing!"

Freud took him to the wall, showed him the switch. He tried it, turned it on and off, and laughed. And he said, "Such a simple thing, and the whole night I tried and could not find it!"

He could have tried his whole life and might have never connected the switch with the light.

This is how it is happening to you; your mind is continuously on. They say that the mind is such a magnificent mechanism that it starts working the moment you are born and it goes on working till you stand before an audience—then suddenly it stops, then something happens to it. Otherwise it continues till you die. And very few people need to stand before an audience, so the mind continues unhindered and it keeps you utterly tired, exhausted, weary, bored. And it goes on saying the same things again and again.

Why are people so bored? Life is not boring, remember. Life is always a tremendous mystery, it is always a surprise, it is always new, it is constantly renewing itself. New leaves are coming, old leaves are falling; new flowers are appearing, old flowers disappearing. But you cannot see life because you are constantly bored by your own mind. It goes on saying things it has said thousands of times. You look so tired, for the simple reason that you don't know how to switch it off.

The mind has not to be thrown out, the mind has to be put in its place. It is a beautiful servant but a very ugly master. Take the reins in your hands, be the master—and the first act, the first step, is to become detached from the mind. See that it is not you, create the distance; the greater the distance the greater is the ability to turn it off.

> Life is always a surprise, it is always new. But you cannot see life because you are constantly bored by your own mind. It goes on saying things it has said thousands of times. You look so tired for the simple reason that you don't know how to switch it off.

And one more miracle you will be coming across is that when you turn the mind off, the mind becomes fresher and more intelligent. Just think: From the day you are born the mind starts and it goes on working till you die—and one never knows, it may even be working when you are in the grave, because a few things continue to happen then. Nails go on growing even when you are in the grave, hair goes on growing, so some kind of mechanism still continues. Even in a dead body the nails and hair go on growing, so something is still working. Maybe there is some local mechanism, not the mind itself, but maybe the body has small, local minds to support the big mind—like agents of the big mind. Maybe these small agents have not yet come to know that the big guy is dead and they go on doing the old thing! They know nothing else so they continue to repeat their old job. Hairs go on growing, nails go on growing—and just small, local minds, miniminds!

The mind has to be put in its right place, and be used only when you need it. Just as you use your legs when you need them—when you don't need to, you don't use your legs. If you are sitting in a chair and you go on moving your legs up and down, then people will think you are mad. That's exactly what is happening in the mind, and still you think you are not mad?

A meditative awareness comes to know the key. Whenever it wants to turn the mind off it simply says, "Now shut up," and that's it. The mind simply keeps quiet and great silence prevails inside. And the mind can also rest in those moments; otherwise everything becomes tired.

Everything tires, everything gets tired—even metals get tired. And your mind is made of very delicate tissues, so delicate that there is nothing more delicate in the whole of existence. In your small skull, millions of small fibers are functioning. They are so thin that your hairs, when compared with the nerves that function in your brain, are very thick, hundreds of thousands of times thicker. Such a delicate phenomenon, but we don't know how to use it. It needs rest.

Hence a meditative person becomes more intelligent, he becomes saner. Whatever he does there is an art in it. Whatever he touches, is transformed into gold.

Mind is a blessing with meditation, otherwise it is a curse. Add meditation to your being and the curse disappears, and the curse itself becomes the blessing; it is a blessing in disguise.

BEING SIMPLE

Simplicity is to live without ideals. Ideals create complexity; ideals create division in you and hence complexity. The moment you are interested in becoming somebody else you become complex. To be contented with yourself as you are is simplicity. The future brings complexity; when you are utterly in the present you are simple.

Simplicity does not mean to live a life of poverty. That is utterly stupid because the person who imposes a life of poverty on himself is not simple at all. He is a hypocrite. The need to impose poverty means, deep down, he hankers for the diametrically opposite; otherwise why should there be any need to impose it? You impose a certain character upon yourself because you are just the opposite of it.

The angry person wants to become compassionate; the violent person wants to become nonviolent. If you are nonviolent you will not try to become nonviolent. For what? The person who imposes poverty upon himself is simply trying to live out a life according to others, not according to his own innermost core, not according to his own spontaneity. And to live according to others is never to be simple.

To live according to others means to live a life of imitation. It will be a plastic life: You will be one thing on the surface and just the opposite of it in your depths. And only the depths matter, the surface never matters. You will be a saint on the surface and a sinner deep down. And that's what is going to be decisive about you because God is only in contact with your depth, not with your surface.

The surface is in contact with the society, the existence is in contact with the depth. The existence only knows what you are, it never knows what you are pretending. The existence never knows about your acts.

You may be pretending to be a great saint, a mahatma, but existence will never know about it, because it never knows about anything false. Anything false happens out of existence. It knows only the real, the real you.

Simplicity means to be just yourself, whosoever you are, in tremendous acceptance, with no goal, with no ideal. All ideals are crap—scrap all of them.

It needs guts to be simple. It needs guts because you will be in constant rebellion. It needs guts because you will never be adjusted to the so-called rotten society that exists around you. You will constantly be an outsider. But you will be simple, and simplicity has beauty. You will be utterly in harmony with yourself. There will be no conflict within you, there will be no split within you.

The ideal brings the split. The bigger the ideal, the bigger is going to be the split. The ideal means somewhere in the future one day, maybe in this life or another life, you will be a great saint. Meanwhile you are a sinner. It helps you to go on hoping; it helps you to go on believing in the surface, that tomorrow everything will be okay, that tomorrow you will be as you should be. The today can be tolerated. You can ignore it, you need not note it, you need not take any notice of it. The real thing is going to be tomorrow.

> Simplicity means to be just yourself, whosoever you are, in tremendous acceptance, with no goal, with no ideal. All ideals are crap—scrap all of them.

But the tomorrow never comes. It is always today . . . it is always today.

And the person who lives in ideals goes on missing reality because reality is now, here. To be now and to be here is to be simple: to be like trees, herenow, to be like clouds, herenow, to be like birds, herenow—to be like buddhas, herenow. The ideal needs the future. Simplicity is not an ideal. People have made an ideal out of simplicity, too; such is human stupidity.

Simplicity can never be an ideal, because no ideal can create simplicity. It is the ideal which poisons you and makes you complex, divides you, makes two persons in you—the one that you are and the one that you would like to be. Now there is going to be a constant war, a civil war.

And when you are fighting with yourself—the violent person trying to be nonviolent, the ugly person trying to be beautiful, and so on, so forth—when you are constantly trying, endeavoring to be something that you are not, your energy is dissipated in that conflict, your energy goes on leaking. And energy is delight. And to have energy is to be alive, to be fresh, to be young.

Look at people's faces, how dull they appear. Look into their eyes, their eyes have lost all luster and all depth. Feel their presence and you will not feel any radiance, you will not feel any energy streaming from them. On the contrary you will feel as if they are sucking you. Rather then overflowing with energy, they have become black holes: They suck you, they exploit your energy. Being with them you will become poorer. That's why when you go into a crowd and come back you feel tired, weary, you feel exhausted, you need rest. Why? Why after being in a crowd do you feel as if you have lost something? You certainly lose something, because the crowd consists of black holes. And the more unintelligent the crowd is, the more of a mob it is, the more you will feel exhausted.

That's why when you are alone, sitting silently, not with anybody—in a tremendous celibate state, just alone—one becomes replenished, rejuvenated. That's why meditation makes you younger, makes you livelier. You start sharing something with existence. Your energy is frozen no more; it starts flowing. You are in a kind of dance, as stars are. A song arises in you.

But in the crowd you always lose. In meditation you always gain. Why? What happens in meditation? In meditation you become simple: The future is your concern no more. That's what meditation is all about: dropping the concern with past and future, being herenow. Only this

131

moment exists. And whenever it happens, whenever only this moment exists—watching a sunrise, or looking at a white cloud floating in the sky, or just being with a tree, silently communing, or observing a bird on the wing—whenever you forget all about past and future and the present moment takes possession of you, when you are utterly possessed by this moment, you will feel rejuvenated. Why? The split disappears, the split created by the ideals. You are one in that moment, integrated; you are all together.

> Whenever you forget all about past and future and the present moment takes possession of you, when you are utterly possessed by this moment, you will feel rejuvenated. Why? The split disappears, the split created by the ideals. You are one in that moment, integrated.

Simplicity is not an ideal; you cannot impose simplicity on yourself. That's why I never say that people like Mahatma Gandhi are simple. They are not, they cannot be. Simplicity is their ideal, they are trying to attain it. Simplicity is a goal far away in the future, distant, and they are striving, they are straining, they are in great effort. How can you create simplicity out of effort? Simplicity simply means that which is. Out of effort you are trying to improve upon existence.

Existence is perfect as it is, it needs no improvement. The so-called saints go on constantly improving upon themselves— drop this, drop that, repress this, impose that, this is not good, that is good . . . Continuous effort, and in this very effort they are lost.

Simplicity is a state of effortlessness; it is humbleness—not the humbleness created against arrogance, not humbleness created against the ego, not humbleness opposite to the proud mind. No, humbleness is not opposite to pride. Humbleness is simply absence of pride. Try to see the point. If your humbleness is against your pride, if you have strived to drop your pride, your ego, your arrogance, then what you have done is only repression. Now you will become proud about your humbleness; now you will start bragging, how humble you are. This is what happens. Just see the so-called humble people—they are constantly broadcasting that they are humble.

The really humble people will not know that they are humble; how can they then brag about it? How can the humble person know that he is humble? The humble person is a person no more. The humble person is in a state of fana: The humble person has dissolved. Now he is only a presence. Humbleness is a presence, not a characteristic of personality, not a trait, but just a presence. Others will feel it, but you will not be able to feel it yourself. So is the case with simplicity.

Simplicity simply means living moment to moment spontaneously, not according to some philosophy, not according to Jainism, Buddhism, Hinduism, not according to any philosophy. Whenever you live according to a philosophy you have betrayed yourself, you are an enemy to yourself. Simplicity means to be in a deep friendship with oneself, to live your life with no idea interfering.

It needs guts, certainly, because you will be living constantly in insecurity. The man who lives with ideals is secure. He is predictable; that is his security. He knows what he is going to do tomorrow. He knows, if a certain situation arises, this is the way he will react to it. He is always certain. The man who is simple knows nothing about tomorrow, knows nothing about the next moment, because he is not going to act out of his past. He will respond out of his present awareness.

The simple person has no "character," only the complex person has character. Good or bad, that is not the point. There are good characters and bad characters, but both are complex. The simple person is characterless, he is neither good nor bad, but he has a beauty which no good people, no bad people can ever have. And the good and the bad are not very different; they are aspects of the same coin. The good person is bad behind it and the bad person is good behind it.

You will be surprised to know that saints always dream that they are committing sins. If you look into the dreams of your so-called saints you will be very much surprised. What kinds of dreams do they go on seeing? That is their suppressed mind that bubbles up, surfaces into their dreams. Sinners always dream that they have become saints. Sinners have the most beautiful dreams, because they have been committing sins their whole life. They are tired of all those things. Now the denied part starts speaking to them in their dreams.

In dreams the denied part speaks to you, your unconscious speaks to you: The unconscious is the denied part. Remember, if you are good in your conscious, if you have cultivated good characteristics in your conscious, you will be bad: All that you have denied will become your unconscious, and vice versa.

The simple person has no conscious, no unconscious; he has no division. He is simply aware. His whole house is full of light. His whole being knows only one thing: awareness. He has not denied anything, hence he has not created the unconscious. This is something to be understood.

Sigmund Freud and Carl Gustav Jung and Alfred Adler and others think that the conscious and unconscious are something natural. They are not. The unconscious is a by-product of civilization. The more a person is civilized, the bigger an unconscious he has, because civilization means repression. Repression means you are denying a few parts of your being from coming into light, you are pushing them into darkness, you are throwing them into your basement so that you never come across them.

People have thrown their sex, their anger, their violence, into the basement and they have locked the doors. But violence, sex, and anger and things like that cannot be locked up. They are like ghosts. They can pass through the walls, there is no way to prevent them. If you succeed in preventing them in your daytime, they will come in the night—they will haunt you in your dreams.

It is because of the unconscious that people dream. The more civilized a person, the more he dreams. Go to the aboriginals, the natural people—a few are still in existence—and you will be again surprised to know that they don't dream much, very rarely, once in a while. Years pass and they never report any dreaming. They simply sleep, without dreams, because they have not repressed anything. They have been living naturally.

The simple person will not have the unconscious, the simple person will not have dreams, but the complex person will have dreams.

That's what happens to you. If you have a fast one day, in the night you will have a feast in your dreams. The fast creates the feast in the dream. And the people who are feasting in the day may start thinking of fasting; they always think about it. It is only rich countries which become interested in fasting. America is interested in fasting, dieting, and all things like that. A poor country cannot think of fasting. A poor country is always fasting, always dieting, always undernourished. Only rich people think of fasting. In India, Jainas are the richest community; their religion consists of fasting. Mohammedans are the poorest, their religion consists of feasting. When a poor man celebrates a religious day he gives a feast. When a rich man celebrates his religious day he fasts.

You can see the logic in it. We go on compensating. The dream is compensatory, it compensates your waking life. The simple man will not dream, the simple man will not have any unconscious.

The simple man will be simple. He will live moment to moment with no idea how to live; he will not have any philosophy of life. He will trust in his intelligence. What is the need of having a philosophy? Why should one have a philosophy? So that it can guide you. It means if you are stupid you need a philosophy of life so that it can guide you. If you are intelligent you don't need any

> Why should one have a philosophy of life? So that it can guide you. If you are intelligent you don't need any philosophy of life. Intelligence is enough unto itself, a light unto itself.

philosophy of life. Intelligence is enough unto itself, a light unto itself.

A blind man asks for guidance: "Where is the door? In what direction should I move? Where is the turn?" Only the blind man prepares himself before he takes any move. The man who has eyes simply moves because he can see. When the door comes he will know and when the turn comes he will know. He can trust in his eyes.

And that is the case with the inner world, too. Trust in your intelligence, don't trust in philosophies of life; otherwise you will remain stupid. The major part of humanity has remained unintelligent because it has trusted in philosophies of life—Christian, Hindu, Mohammedan.

Again, something of very great importance to be remembered: Each child is born intelligent. Intelligence is not something that a few have and a few don't have. Intelligence is the fragrance of life itself. Life has it—if you are alive you are intelligent. But then if you never trust in it, it starts slowly, slowly disappearing from your life. If you don't use your legs you will lose the capacity to run. If you don't use your eyes for three years and you remain with a blindfold you will become blind. You can keep your senses alive only if you go on continuously using them.

Intelligence is a natural phenomenon; every child is born intelligent. Very few people live intelligently, and very few people die intelligently. Ninety-nine point nine percent of people remain stupid their whole life—and they were not unintelligent in the beginning. So what happens? They never use their intelligence. When they are small children they trust their parents and their guidance.

In a better world the parents, if they really love their children, will teach them to trust their own intelligence. In a better world the parents will help the children to be independent as soon as possible, to be on their own.

Then, they have to trust the teachers in the school; then the professors in the college and in the university. By the time one-third of their life is gone, they come out of the university utterly stupid. One-third of their life they have been taught to trust somebody else: that's how their intelligence has been prevented from functioning.

Look at small children, how intelligent they are, how alive, how fresh, how tremendously ready to learn. And look at older people, dull, insipid, not ready to learn a thing, clinging to all that they know, clinging to the known, never ready to go on any adventure.

In a better world children will be thrown upon themselves as soon as possible; the whole effort of the parents should be to make the child use his intelligence. And the whole effort, if education is right—if it is education and not *mis*education—will be to throw the child again and again back to his own intelligence so that he can function, so that he can use it. He may not be so efficient in the beginning, that is true—the teacher may have the right answer, and if the student has to work out his own answer the answer may not be so right—but that is not the point at all. The answer may not be so right, it may not correspond to the answers given in the books, but it will be intelligent. And that is the real crux of the matter.

Watch children and you will be constantly surprised. But we start destroying their intelligence because we are too concerned about the right answer—not the intelligent answer, but the right answer. That is a wrong concern. Let the answer be intelligent, let the answer be a little bit original, let the answer be the child's own. Don't be bothered about the right, don't be in such a hurry; the right will come on its own. Let the child search for it, let him stumble upon it on his own. Why are we in such a hurry?

We simply drop the child's growth of intelligence; we supply the right answer. Just think: The whole process is that the child is never allowed to find the answer himself. We give him the answer. When the answer is given from the outside, intelligence need not grow, because intelligence only grows when it has to find the answer itself.

But we are so obsessed with the idea of the right. No wrong should ever be committed. Why not? And the person who never commits any wrong never grows. Growth needs that you should go astray sometimes, that you should start playing around, fooling around, that you should find original things, even though they may be wrong. You should come to the right by your own efforts, by your own growth; then there is intelligence.

137

To be simple means to be intelligent. Simplicity is intelligence, living without ideals, without guides, without maps, just living moment to moment without any security.

> ☙
>
> Growth needs that you should go astray sometimes, that you should start playing around, fooling around, that you should find original things—they may be wrong, and you should come to the right by your own efforts, by your own growth, then there is intelligence.

Our concern with the right and our fear of the wrong is nothing but our fear of the insecure. The right makes us secure, the wrong makes us insecure, but life is insecurity. There is no security anywhere. You may have a bank balance, but the bank can go bankrupt any day. You may have the security of having a husband or a wife, but the wife can leave you any moment, she can fall in love; or the husband may die.

Life is insecure. Security is only an illusion that we create around ourselves, a cozy illusion. And because of this cozy illusion we kill our intelligence. The man who wants to live simply will have to live in insecurity, will have to accept the fact that nothing is secure and certain, that we are on an unknown journey, that nobody can be certain where we are going and nobody can be certain from where we are coming.

In fact, except for the stupid people nobody has illusions of certainty. The more intelligent you are, the more uncertain you are. The more intelligent you are, the more hesitant—because life is vast. Life is immense, immeasurable, mysterious. How can you be certain?

Living in uncertainty, living in insecurity, is simplicity. Living a life without ideals, without character, a life not rooted in the past, not motivated by the future; a life utterly here and now.

138

A LIGHT UNTO YOURSELF

The last words of Gautama the Buddha on the earth were: *Be a light unto yourself*. Do not follow others, do not imitate, because imitation, following, creates stupidity. You are born with a tremendous possibility of intelligence. You are born with a light within you. <u>Listen to the still, small voice within, and that will guide you</u>. Nobody else can guide you, nobody else can become a model for your life, because you are unique. There has never been anyone who was exactly like you, and nobody is ever again going to be exactly like you. This is your glory, your grandeur—that you are utterly irreplaceable, that you are just yourself and nobody else.

The person who follows others becomes false, he becomes pseudo, he becomes mechanical. He can be a great saint in the eyes of others, but deep down, he is simply unintelligent and nothing else. He may have a very respectable character but that is only on the surface, it is not even skin-deep. Scratch him a little and you will be surprised that inside he is a totally different person, just the opposite of his outside.

By following others you can cultivate a beautiful character, but you cannot have a beautiful consciousness, and unless you have a beautiful consciousness you can never be free. You can go on changing your prisons, you can go on changing your bondages, your slaveries. You can be a Hindu or a Mohammedan or a Christian or a Jaina—that is not going to help you.

> By following others you can cultivate a beautiful character, but you cannot have a beautiful consciousness, and unless you have a beautiful consciousness you can never be free.

To be a Jaina means to follow Mahavira as the model. Now, there is nobody who is like Mahavira or ever can be. Following Mahavira, you will become a false entity. You will lose all reality, you will lose all sincerity, you will be untrue to yourself. You will become artificial, unnatural, and to be artificial, to be unnatural, is the way of the mediocre, the stupid, the fool.

Buddha defines wisdom as living in the light of your own consciousness, and he defines foolishness as following others, imitating others, becoming a shadow to somebody else.

The real master creates masters, not followers. The real master throws you back to yourself. His whole effort is to make you independent of him, because you have been dependent for centuries, and it has not led you anywhere. You still continue to stumble in the dark night of the soul.

Only your inner light can become the sunrise. The false master persuades you to follow him, to imitate him, to be just a carbon copy of him. The real master will not allow you to be a carbon copy, he wants you to be the original. He loves you! How can he make you imitative? He has compassion for you, he would like you to be utterly free—free from all outer dependencies.

> One has to go through life unprotected; one has to seek and search one's way. Life is an opportunity, a challenge, to find yourself.

But the ordinary human being does not want to be free. He wants to be dependent. He wants somebody else to guide him. Why? Because then he can throw the whole responsibility on the shoulders of somebody else. And the more responsibility you throw away onto somebody else's shoulders, the smaller the possibility of your ever becoming intelligent. It is responsibility, the challenge of responsibility, that creates wisdom.

One has to accept life with all its problems. One has to go through life unprotected; one has to seek and search one's way. Life is an opportunity, a challenge, to find yourself. But the fool does not want to go the hard way, the fool chooses the shortcut. He says to himself, "Buddha has attained—why should I bother? I will just watch his behavior and imitate it. Jesus has attained, so why should I search and seek? I can simply become a shadow to Jesus. I can simply go on following him wherever he goes."

But by following somebody else, how are you going to become intelligent? You will not provide any chance for your intelligence to explode. It needs a challenging life, an adventurous life, a life that knows how to risk and how to go into the unknown, for intelligence to arise. And only intelligence can save you—nobody else. Your own intelligence, mind you, your own awareness, can become your nirvana.

Be a light unto yourself and you will be wise; let others become your leaders, your guides, and you will remain stupid, and you will go on missing all the treasures of life—which were yours.

SYMPTOMS, STEPPING-STONES, AND STUMBLING BLOCKS

RESPONSES TO QUESTIONS

Can computers take over the work of human intelligence?

The question may not appear very serious, but it is one of the most serious questions possible. The first thing to remember is that it is going to happen. There is no possibility to avoid it; neither is there any need to avoid it. Perhaps I am the only one in the world who is in absolute support of mechanical brains taking over the work of human intelligence. The reasons are very clear, why I am in support of such a strange thing.

First, what we call the human mind is itself a biocomputer. Just because you are born with it does not make much difference. A better computer can be implanted in your mind—far more efficient, far more intelligent, far more comprehensive.

There are always people who are afraid of every new thing. Every new thing has been opposed by religions, by churches vehemently, because every new thing changes the whole structure of human life. For example, the computer can change all the stupidity that man has shown through the whole of history. I don't think that computers will like to create war, or computers will exploit people, or computers will discriminate between black and white, between man and woman.

Moreover, you are always the master, not the computer. You can always change the program of the computer. The computer is simply a tremendous instrument, which gives you immense possibilities that are not available to you biologically. You can do things which man has never dreamt of. The computer can be a thousand times more superior than Albert Einstein. Naturally the computer can produce a science far more fundamental, far more real, not changing every day because new discoveries go on happening and the old discovery becomes out of date. The computer can reach the very center of reality.

It can reveal to you whatever you want. It is an instrument in your hands. It is not a danger.

And because it will be doing all the intellectual, mental work, nobody has seen the possibility that I am telling you, that you will be left very simply to relax into meditation. The computer can be put to the side. The computer can do all the thinking; you need not go on continuously chattering unnecessarily. And the computer is not Christian, is not Hindu, is not Mohammedan. It is simply a mechanical device created by human consciousness. And in return it can help human consciousness to reach its highest potential.

But every new thing will be opposed, because every new thing will make old things out of date. Old factories will close, old industries will close. There are many inventions that are never marketed in the world because the people whose business will be affected by them purchase their patents. And the scientist has not the money to make his own conception into a reality.

There are hundreds of inventions that can help humanity to be more comfortable, to be more joyous, to have better clothes, better food. But they will not ever come to light because there are people who are going to be ruined if those new things come onto the market. And new things naturally create fear.

But today, many factories are run by robots. They never tire, they never retire; they don't ask for a salary or for a raise; they don't form unions, they don't go on strike. They are the nicest people you can find.

And they work twenty-four hours, day in, day out. Their efficiency is perfect, a hundred percent. But it is a danger because people are becoming unemployed. Now these unemployed people are going to create trouble; they don't want robots. But I am all in favor of robots. Everybody should be unemployed and paid—paid for being unemployed. Robots are doing the work, you get the pay. And life becomes sheer joy.

> *If the whole world is unemployed and has enough money to enjoy, do you think anybody is going to join the army? People will join carnivals, circuses . . . All kinds of celebrations will happen, but there is no need for war.*

Then you can meditate, you can dance, you can sing, you can go for world trips. The problem arises because we cannot think of the solution. The solution is simple. You were paid because you were producing. Now the robot is producing more, much more efficiently, and he is not being paid. There is no need for you to remain unemployed, hungry, poor. It is such simple arithmetic: You should be paid—paid more because now you have vacated the place for a robot that produces a hundred times more. So if your salary is doubled there is no loss.

And if the whole world is unemployed and has enough money to enjoy, do you think anybody is going to join the army? People will join carnivals, circuses . . . All kinds of celebrations will happen, but there is no need for war. And even if war is an absolute necessity, robots are there, just let them fight. Nobody is going to win. Both sides are robots; nobody is going to be killed. Every day they come back with a few parts missing; repair them and send them back. Even war can become a great joy—there will be no question of defeat or victory.

But people are afraid because they cannot conceive of a world in which people don't suffer. Your concern is that these computers are going to take the place of intelligence. They will be far superior in intelligence, but remember one thing: Those computers are in your hands. You are not in their hands, so there is no problem.

Up to now you have lived according to memory, which is an unnecessary burden, carrying it in your head. Twenty-five years of teaching in the schools, colleges, universities; Ph.D.s, D.Litt.s . . . What are you doing? You are creating a computer, but with an old, out-of-date method—forcing small children to memorize. There is no need. The computer can do everything, it just has to be given information.

You can buy a computer that knows everything about medical science. You need not go to a medical college; you simply ask the computer and immediately the answer is there. Your memory is not so reliable. And the computer can always be fed with new memory, because new discoveries are being made every day. The computer can be plugged into the main computer of the university, so without your even bothering, every new discovery concerning your subject is immediately fed into your computer. It waits there, you make an inquiry, and the computer tells you.

You can have a multidimensional computer which has all kinds of memory, or a one-dimensional computer which has only history, the whole history of mankind. Now, you cannot have the whole history of mankind. Do you know on what date Socrates was married to Xanthippe? The computer can tell you immediately. That unfortunate date . . . I have always suspected that Socrates accepted the poison so easily because of his wife, because life was so torturous—death cannot be worse than that.

How much can you memorize? Your memory has a limitation. But the computer can memorize almost unlimited amounts of things. And there are many more possibilities: One computer can join together with another computer and manage to figure out new inventions, new medicines, new ways of health, new ways of living.

Computers should not be taken as monsters. They are a great blessing. And what man's intellect has done is very small. Once the computer takes over, so much can be done that there will be no need for anybody to be hungry, no need for anybody to be poor, no need for anybody to be a thief, no need for anybody to be a judge, because these all belong to the same profession—judges and thieves, criminals and lawmakers. There is no need for anybody to be poor and no need for anybody to be rich. Everybody can be affluent.

But perhaps no government will allow this to happen. No religion will allow this to happen, because it will go against their scriptures, it will go against their doctrines. Hindus believe that you have to suffer because in your past life you committed evil acts. Nobody knows about past lives. They cannot accept an invention which can remove misery, poverty, sickness, because then what will happen to the theory of reincarnation, and rewards and punishments of good and bad deeds? The whole doctrine of Hinduism will be simply meaningless.

A young man came from the university with the degree of M.D. His old father was waiting for him, because he was tired, working his whole life. Three of his sons were studying at medical college—if at least one comes back, he can take his place and support the other two. And the young man immediately said, "You need not be worried. You rest and relax, I will take care."

And the third day he approached his father and said, "Dad, the woman you have been treating for thirty years I have cured."

The father said, "You idiot! That is the woman who has paid for your education and was paying for your two other brothers. I was keeping her in this condition. She was so rich she could afford to be sick. She was not poor."

To be rich and to be sick is very dangerous. To be poor and to be sick is not very dangerous. You will be cured very soon, because you cannot pay much. On the contrary, you may ask the doctor, "What about the medicine, what about the food you have prescribed? I don't have any money." The doctor will think, "It is better to cure him and get rid of him." But when a rich man is sick, then it becomes professionally a very strange dilemma in the mind of the physician: to cure him or to have him linger on—because the more he lingers on, the more money you get. If you cure him, you don't get that money.

But if computers can manage, then many professions will be affected. And these will be the professions that will prevent it; they will make a thousand and one excuses: God never created a computer, computers are dangerous because they will take all intelligence away from you.

What are you doing with your intelligence? Being miserable, being jealous? At least computers will not be jealous and will not be miserable. What are you doing with your intelligence? Destructiveness, all kinds of wars, all kinds of violence.

> ⤍
>
> What are you doing with your intelligence? Being miserable, being jealous? At least computers will not be jealous and will not be miserable.

Computers can give you a complete holiday for your whole life. You can relax. You will have to learn how to relax, because you have all become workaholics. For thousands of years, work, work, work hard! Computers will go against your whole conditioning about work. Laziness will become for the first time a spiritual quality: Blessed are the laziest, for theirs is the kingdom of this planet. And in their laziness, if they want, they can make beautiful gardens. It is just out of joy, for no purpose. They can paint—not to sell, but just to rejoice in the colors, the mixing of colors, the dance of colors. They can play music—not for any monetary reason, not as a business, but simply as a playful joy.

What man has dreamt of finding in paradise, life can really become here on this planet. There is no need to go that far. And nobody knows the way and nobody has ever gone there. And those who have gone have not even dropped a card: "We have arrived!" Such miserly people—just a Christmas card . . . But paradise has to be created; there is no paradise in existence. It has to come out of man's awareness, consciousness.

The computer is also part of man's creativity. There is no need to become a competitor; you are the master. And for the first time the computer and you are separate. That's what all the teachings of the mystics have been telling you, that your mind and you are separate. But it is difficult because the mind is inside your head and your consciousness is so close to it, so thousands of mystics have been teaching this but nobody listens. The distance is not very great. But with computers, the distance will be very clear; there will be no need for any mystic to tell you.

Everybody has his own computer in his pocket and knows that it is separate. And one is free from thinking—the computer is doing it. You want to think something, tell the computer to think it. If your old habit of chattering arises, tell the computer, "Chatter," and it will chatter. But you can be for the first time what the buddhas have been talking about—just aware, silent, peaceful, a pool of consciousness.

A computer cannot be aware. A computer can be intellectual, a computer can be knowledgeable; a computer can be so knowledgeable that it can contain all the information of all the libraries in the whole world—a single computer that you can keep in your pocket. It will relieve millions of people from memorizing unnecessary things. It will keep millions of people from teaching and torturing students. Examinations and all kinds of stupid things will disappear.

The computer can be one of the greatest phenomena that has ever happened. It can become the quantum leap. It can break away from the past and all conditionings of the past.

Hymie Goldberg answers a classified advertisement in a newspaper which says, "Opportunity of a lifetime!" He is given an address and finds himself face to face with old man Finkelstein.

"What I am looking for," explains old man Fink, "is somebody to do all my worrying for me. Your job will be to shoulder all my cares."

"That's quite a job," says Hymie. "How much do I get paid?"

"You will get twenty thousand dollars a year," says old man Fink, "to make every worry of mine your own."

"Okay," says Hymie, "when do I get paid?"

"Aha!" says Fink. "That's your first worry."

Why does humanity seem so willing to walk the path toward global suicide?

The reason is clear. People have realized that their life has no meaning, that except for misery, nothing happens; except for anxiety, anguish, life has nothing to offer.

Individuals have always committed suicide. And you will be surprised: The people who have committed suicide have always been a little more intelligent than the normal people. Psychologists commit suicide twice as much as any other profession. Painters, poets, philosophers either go mad or commit suicide. Idiots have never been known to commit suicide, nor do they go mad.

The idiots have never committed suicide because they cannot even think about meaning, significance, purpose. They don't think at all; they simply live, they vegetate. The higher the intelligence, the more dangerous, because it makes you aware that the life that you are living is just hollow, utterly empty. There is nothing to hold on to. You know tomorrow will be a repetition of today, so what is the point of continuing?

Individuals have committed suicide because only individuals have come to a certain stage of intelligence, of understanding whether life has any meaning or not. Now, for the first time, millions of people around the earth have reached that maturity where they feel life is meaningless. That's why humanity is moving toward a global suicide. There seems to be no reason to continue—for what? You have lived your life, and you have found nothing. Now your children will live and they will find nothing: generation after generation, only emptiness in your hands—no fulfillment, no contentment.

> For the first time, millions of people around the earth have reached that maturity where they feel life is meaningless. That's why humanity is moving toward a global suicide. There seems to be no reason to continue—for what?

But to me, this gives man a tremendous opportunity. Only very highly intelligent people have committed suicide or have become mad, because they could not live with this insane world. They could not adapt themselves to all kinds of insanities that are going around. They felt themselves fallen apart—that was their madness. But only the same kind of people have also become enlightened.

So these are the three possibilities for intelligence. Either the intelligent person goes mad because he cannot figure out what is happening, why it is happening, why he is supposed to do this or that. Or, seeing the situation, that it is driving him mad, he commits suicide, he puts an end to life. This has been mostly the case in the West.

In the East the same kind of people have tried something else—not madness, but meditation. The West is poor in that way. It does not know the richness of meditation. It does not know that meditation can transform your whole vision of life; it can give you tremendous meaningfulness, beauty, benediction. Then life is something sacred, you cannot destroy it.

You must look at it, that in the East the rate of suicide is very low compared to the West, the rate of people going mad is very low compared to the West. And one thing more: In the East, the people who go mad are really not very intelligent people. They are psychologically sick. It is not their intelligence that has led them to madness, it is something missing in their minds. Perhaps their food is not right, it is not enough to help their mind become mature. Their vegetarianism is lacking certain proteins which are absolutely needed for intelligence to grow.

So the madness in the West and in the East is totally different. The madness in the East is something psychological: They are missing certain things, their growth is retarded, their minds cannot grow the way they would have grown.

The people who commit suicide in the East are also different from the people who commit suicide in the West. In the East people commit suicide because of hunger, because of starvation, because they cannot manage to live—and life becomes such a torture. So there is a qualitative difference.

But the intelligent people in the East have always turned toward meditation. Whenever they have felt that life has no meaning, they have tried to find the meaning within themselves; that's the way of meditation. They have tried to find out the very source of life, love, and they have found it. Anybody who looks inward is bound to find it. It is not far away, it is just within you. You are carrying it all the time!

The Western intelligentsia is looking for meaning outside, and there is no meaning outside. They are looking for blissfulness outside. Remember, the beauty is in the eyes of the onlooker; it is not there outside. And the same is true about meaningfulness, blissfulness, benediction. It is within your vision, it is within you. When you have it, you can project it over the whole of existence. But first you have to find it within yourself.

> Intelligent people in the East have always turned toward meditation. Whenever they have felt that life has no meaning, they have tried to find the meaning within themselves, that's the way of meditation.

If Jean-Paul Sartre, Marcel Proust, Martin Heidegger, Ludwig Wittgenstein, Bertrand Russell, people like these, had been born in the

East, they would all have become enlightened beings. But in the West, they all became tremendously burdened with anguish, anxiety. They found that it is all accidental and meaningless, that there is no purpose in life, and joy is just a dream, just a hope; it does not exist in reality.

The West needs meditation. The East needs medicine; it is sick in the body. The West is sick in the soul. Once we understand the problem clearly . . . Now it is not the East which is a danger to the world; at the most they can starve and die as they are dying in Ethiopia. But it is not a danger to the world. In fact, in a way the starving East is helping the world by dying. It is reducing the population of the world. It is making everybody richer, without your knowing it. One thousand Ethiopians dying every day—you may not see that somehow they are helping your comfort, but they are, because if the population of the world is reduced, people can live more comfortably, more easily, more joyously.

The problem is not coming from the East; the problem is coming from the West. The problem is that the Western intelligentsia is fed up with life, so there is no real resistance from the intelligentsia against nuclear weapons, against a third world war. In fact, it seems deep down the Western mind is somehow hoping that it happens soon, because life is meaningless.

Rather than taking the risk of committing suicide yourself, if politicians can manage to destroy the whole world, that will be far easier. You will not be in the dilemma of to be or not to be. You will not have to think whether to destroy yourself or not, to wonder if perhaps tomorrow things may be different.

It is an individual responsibility to commit suicide, but a global war, a nuclear war—all your personal responsibility disappears. It is not your doing, it is just happening.

Why is the Western intelligentsia not really fighting against nuclear weapons? Why are the scientists—who are part of the intelligentsia—still serving governments? The simplest way would be for all the scientists who are creating nuclear weapons to resign. They should say, "Enough is enough. We cannot create these weapons which are going to destroy life on the earth." And the poets, the philosophers, the painters—they don't seem to protest. They have just become spectators. There is a reason behind it. Western humanity has been turned by and by into spectators—about everything.

You don't play football, but twenty-two persons who are professionals, this is their business, to play football. And millions of people are just spectators, and they are so excited . . . jumping in their seats, screaming, shouting. If they are not in the stadium, then they are sitting in their homes before the television screen and they are doing the same gestures there. Somebody else is playing; you are just a spectator.

The average American is looking at the television five to six hours a day: six hours of just being a spectator, not a participant. Then there are movies where you are spectators, and there are boxing matches where you are spectators. It seems you have lost contact with life. You simply see others living; your life is just to watch. Somebody is in a competition for a world championship in chess, and you are watching. Can't you play chess yourself? Can't you play football yourself?

It is not far away, it is already happening . . . you will not be making love to your wife, to your girlfriend—somebody else will be doing it and you will be watching, jumping: "Aha! Great! Go on!"

You have left the whole of life for others to live on your behalf, and then you ask where the meaning has gone, why you don't feel alive, why there is not some significance in your life. Spectators cannot have significance—only participants, totally involved, intensely involved in every action.

So perhaps the Western intelligentsia is just in the situation of spectators, watching when it is announced on the television that the third world war has begun. Listening to the radio, reading the newspaper . . . But are you going to do something or not?

It is *doing* that keeps your juices running. If you are simply watching, your own juices dry up. You become just a skeleton.

I am surprised that the West has a great, educated, intelligent majority in the world, but they do nothing, they don't take any action. AIDS is spreading—you are simply watching. Your governments are piling up nuclear weapons, preparing your funeral pyre—and you are just watching.

You have to be taken out of this hypnotic state of being a mere spectator. There are not many people who are making nuclear weapons. There are only a few scientists who know how. Can't they simply say, "No, we are not going to be servants of death"?

> Unless you start feeling some meaning in life, some joy arising in you, some fragrance surrounding you, you cannot fight for life. And life needs, for the first time in the history of man, to be fought for.

And all the poets and all the painters and all the great Nobel prizewinners, novelists, actors, musicians, dancers—what are they doing? There should be a great protest—all the nuclear weapons should be drowned in the Pacific. Whoever named it the "Pacific" must have had a great insight into the future. Now let that name become a reality.

But the trouble is, unless you start feeling some meaning in life, some joy arising in you, some fragrance surrounding you, you cannot fight for life. And life needs, for the first time in the history of man, to be fought for.

Meditation will create the necessary atmosphere. It will bring you back to action, back to love, back to meaning. And then, naturally, you will see that it is time for something to be done. This beautiful earth should not die.

This is a unique planet, very small. In this immense universe, which knows no limits, this small earth is unique—unique because birds sing here, flowers blossom here, life has reached a new level: consciousness. And in a few people consciousness has touched its omega point: enlightenment.

Compared to this earth, the whole universe is dead. It is big, vast, but even a single rose flower is far more valuable than the biggest stars.

Anybody who wants to destroy this earth wants to destroy something unique that is evolving. And it has taken millennia to come to this state of consciousness. Even if only a few people have attained to ultimate bliss and ecstasy, that is enough to make this earth the greatest treasure.

There are millions of solar systems, but no solar system can claim a Gautam Buddha, a Lao Tzu, a Bodhidharma, a Kabir. This earth has done something immensely great, it has made the whole universe rich. It cannot be destroyed.

War should be stopped—and it is within our hands to do so. Don't be only a spectator. Rather than just remaining in your misery, start finding sources of life and mystery within yourself. That is the only possibility for saving the whole world.

I cannot cope with many social situations I find myself in. Do I need the help of a psychiatrist?

Your mind is perfectly okay. In fact, this situation happens to everybody who has a certain intelligence. It is not that you are lacking something, it is that you have more than average intelligence. This problem is not because of lack, this problem is because of something plus: You have more intelligence than average.

When the mind is a little more intelligent it is never satisfied because it can always imagine better situations; that is the problem. If you have one thousand rupees and you are stupid you can he satisfied! But how can an intelligent man be satisfied? He thinks of two thousand, three thousand, five thousand; whatsoever he has he can always imagine more.

You have a beautiful woman; a intelligent person starts thinking of more beautiful women, he goes on fantasizing. An idiot is satisfied because he cannot imagine . . . he cannot even imagine a better situation, so why be unsatisfied, how to be unsatisfied?

So psychiatrists cannot help because you don't have anything wrong! They cannot put anything right because there is nothing wrong. You have more than average intelligence. Now, you will have to apply this intelligence to your problems more deeply. Rather than asking somebody else's help, you will have to apply your own intelligence to your problems.

For example, when you are unsatisfied with a certain thing, become very aware of why you are unsatisfied—see the whole dissatisfaction, go into it deeply. Layer by layer, open all the doors, examine every situation, every mood. Awareness is going to help you because you have intelligence and intelligence can be converted into awareness.

Sermons won't help—somebody saying, "Just be satisfied," is not going to help you; that you cannot do. You will have to go into deep analysis of your own moods. So whenever you are feeling unsatisfied, nothing is wrong—the first thing to be understood is that nothing is wrong! You should feel fortunate because you could have been stupid—stupid people never have this problem, idiots don't have any problems. A problem is a good indication.

And when you think about life, when you become aware of life . . . life is meaningless, so how to be satisfied with it? If you go deeply into this, by and by you will start feeling that in life there is no possibility of any satisfaction. Then you have stumbled upon the first basic truth—that life is meaningless. Then one can turn within; then there is no need to go outside, because outside there is no meaning possible. There is only anxiety and anguish.

And people like you commit suicide. When life becomes too heavy and everything is unsatisfactory and nothing brings happiness, one starts feeling, "What is the point of going on living? Then destroy yourself!" People of your type either commit suicide or they become great seekers; both are possibilities. If they don't destroy themselves they start turning inward and they create a new life. The life that is available through the senses is meaningless, but that is not the only life. There is one more life, far greater, far more glorious, and that is the life of an inward consciousness.

So now you are becoming a seeker, you are at the door of it, so please don't think that you are ill. If you think in those terms you will start feeling ill, you will hypnotize yourself into believing that you are ill. You are not ill at all. Completely drop that idea! Never go to a psychiatrist, because if you go they will find something wrong with you even if it is not there. They have to find it—they also have to live, so when somebody comes they have to find something wrong and treat him.

I can see deeply into you that there is nothing wrong. It is just that you are unfortunate in one way that you have more than average intelligence. So you can make a misery out of it or you can make a blessing out of it—it depends on you.

I feel fed up with myself, feel no connection between my inner world and the outer one. I used to have many interests but no longer feel in touch with them.

This is how any intelligent person will feel. Boredom is the price one pays for intelligence. It should not be taken negatively. This is good, because in understanding this there is a possibility to transcend. If you are not fed up, you can never transcend yourself. Blessed are those who are really fed up because they can transcend. Of course, to transcend is a difficult and arduous job; it is not easy. It is like climbing Everest—it is a difficult thing—but once you are really fed up, then even in the difficulty there is a challenge.

So the first thing is, don't be worried about it—it is good that it is so. And don't take it negatively—it is part of intelligence, and you are an intelligent person, so naturally you are bound to come to this state of boredom.

The second thing . . .

When you start being fed up, naturally you will start wondering how to go inward because you are fed up with the outside, you know all that is outside. I was just reading today a very ancient story of a king—his name was Bhartirhari.

When he became the king, he called all his ministers and told them, "This will be my rule and this is my order to you: I want to experience everything once but never twice. So the same food has not to be served to me again, the same woman has not to be brought to me again—everything just once!"

By the end of the year they came and said, "No more is possible. All that we could do, we have done. Now we are driving ourselves crazy—we cannot find new things!"

The king said, "It is okay—I will renounce it all!" And he became a sannyasin. He said, "Now finished! I have tasted everything once, what is the point of tasting it twice? I am not so stupid! Once is okay—now I know the taste of it—but what is the point of repeating the taste of it?"

I loved the story . . . it is tremendously beautiful.

This is how any intelligent person will be! So there is nothing to be worried about—don't become serious about it. It is good, it is perfectly okay to feel fed up. People who don't feel fed up with themselves are in a wrong situation; they are in danger, they will never change. There is no need for them to change. They will go on revolving in the wheel—they are mechanical people.

> People who don't feel fed up with themselves are in a wrong situation, they are in danger, they will never change.

This is the first ray of consciousness in you—that you feel fed up.

Who is this one who feels fed up? This awareness is you—this is the first ray of consciousness. So the way that you have lived up to now and all the things that you have done up to now are meaningless.

Now, the second thing . . . The problem arises that now the outside is almost finished—how to go inward? If you start struggling to go in, it will not be in. If you try and make an effort to go in, it will not be in, because whatsoever we do with effort leads outside, takes us outside; anything done by effort moves outward.

To go in means to relax, to let go—there is no other way. When you relax you go in, when you start doing something you go out. Doing means going out, nondoing means going in. That's why it is arduous. If there were something to do I would have told you, "Do this and you will be in." It is not a question of doing. You will have to learn patience, you will have to learn infinite patience.

And just start sitting. Whenever you have time just sit silently with closed eyes not doing anything. You are fed up with the outside? By and by the dreams of the outside will disappear because there is no need for the dreams to continue.

You will not think of food—if you think of food, then know well you are not fed up. If you think of women, know well you are not yet fed up. Your dreams will show you whether you are really fed up or if there is still some lingering interest. If a lingering interest is there, then finish that, too; there is no harm in it. If you are really fed up, by and by you will start feeling that the energy is moving inward on its own accord. You are not doing anything, you are simply sitting there and it is going in, it is falling in.

And through that inwardness your centering will arise. Through that inwardness new interests, new enthusiasm, new style, a new way to live will come. You cannot cultivate it—all that you can cultivate will be just a repetition of the old . . . maybe a little modified here and there, but it won't make much difference. So start sitting passively and do more passive meditations.

In my work I am always afraid of losing confidence in myself.

In fact, we don't need as much confidence as we think we need.

Confidence can either be a great quality or it can be a hindrance to some. For example, foolish people are always more confident than intelligent people. Stupidity has a certain confidence to it. Foolish people are more stubborn, and because they are blind, because they can't see, they rush anywhere—even where angels fear to tread.

A person who is intelligent is bound to have a little hesitancy. Intelligence is hesitant. That simply shows that there are millions of opportunities, millions of alternatives, and one has to choose. Every choice is arbitrary, so a certain lack of confidence is bound to be there. The more intelligent you are, the more you will feel it.

So not all confidence is good. Ninety-nine percent of confidence is foolish. Only one percent is good, and that one percent is never absolute. That one percent is always hesitant because there are really so many alternatives. You are always standing at the crossroads, not knowing which road will really be the right one. How can you be confident? Why do you expect to be confident?

All roads look almost the same but one has to choose. It is a gambler's choice. But that's how life is—and it is good that it is that way. If everything was clear-cut, preplanned, prefabricated, and you were just given instructions—"Move right and left and do this and that"—there would be confidence but of what use would it be? The thrill would be lost. There would be no light in life then. It would be a dead routine.

Life is always thrilling because each step brings you to another crossroads . . . again so many roads, again you have to choose. You start trembling. Will the choice be right or not? How to be rightly confident then? To be rightly confident is to think about all the alternatives and whatsoever you feel is a little better than the others . . .

> There are millions of opportunities, millions of alternatives, and one has to choose. Every choice is arbitrary, so a certain lack of confidence is bound to be there. The more intelligent you are, the more you will feel it.

Don't ask for absolute good and absolute wrong. In life there is nothing like that. It is only a percentage; one is only a little better than the other, that's all. Life is not divided like two polarities into good and bad. There are a thousand and one situations between good and bad. So just look around objectively, silently, feelingly, see every possibility, unworried, and whatsoever feels a little bit better than others, move on it. Once you decide to move, forget about other alternatives, because they don't matter now. Then move confidently.

> Just look around objectively, silently, feelingly—see every possibility, unworried, and whatever feels a little bit better than others, move on it. Once you decide to move, forget about other alternatives, because they don't matter now. Then move confidently.

This is really intelligent confidence. It does not destroy hesitation completely. It uses hesitation. It does not destroy alternatives. Alternatives are there. It consciously broods and contemplates over all the alternatives as silently as humanly possible. Intelligence never demands anything inhuman.

These are the paths. Many are moving to the right; they think it is better. You still feel that to move to the left is better, so of course there is going to be hesitation because you know that many intelligent people are moving in the opposite direction. How can you be confident? You are not alone here. Many intelligent people are going that way and still you feel that this is right for you.

Stand on the crossroads, think, meditate, but once you decide then forget all other alternatives—move. Once you decide to move, your whole energy is needed there. Don't be split and don't let half of your mind think about alternatives. This is how one has to use hesitation.

And there is no certainty that you are bound to be right. That I am not saying. There is no way to be certain. You may be wrong, but there is no way to know it unless you follow the road to the very end, all the way.

But my understanding is that one should think rightly. The very thinking gives you growth. You move on the road—right or wrong is irrelevant. The very movement gives you growth. To me it is not a question of where you go. To me the most important thing is that you are not stuck, but going.

Even if this road comes to a dead end and it leads nowhere and you have to come back, nothing to worry about. It is good that you went. The very movement has given you much experience. You have known a wrong road. You are acquainted with wrong now more than before. Now you know what is false; it will help you to find out the truth.

To know the false as false is a great experience because that is the only way that one comes by and by to know what truth is. To know truth as true, the path moves from the experience of knowing false as false. And one has to move on many wrong roads before one comes to the right one.

> To know truth as true, the path moves from the experience of knowing false as false. And one has to move on many wrong roads before one comes to the right one.

So to me, even if you are going toward hell, I bless you because there is no other way to know hell. And if you don't know hell you will never be able to know what heaven is. Go into the dark because that is the way to know light. Go into death because that is the way to know life.

The only thing that is important is not to be stuck somewhere. Don't just stand on the crossroads, hesitating, not going anywhere. Don't make hesitation your habit.

Use it—it is a good device. Think about all the alternatives. I'm not saying don't think, don't hesitate at all. Don't move like a stupid man and run with closed eyes, blindfolded, so there is no problem and you don't know that other roads exist. That's why stupid people are more confident, but they have done much harm in the world. The world would be better if there were fewer confident people.

Look at the Adolf Hitlers—they are very confident. They think God has given them great work to change the whole world. They are stupid people but very confident. Even Buddha is not as confident as Adolf Hitler, because Buddha is not stupid. He understands the complexity of life. It is not so simple as Hitler thinks, but he just rushes and people follow him.

Why do so many people follow such stupid leaders? Why do so many people go on following politicians? What happens? Rarely it happens that a politician is intelligent—because if he is intelligent he will not be a politician. Intelligence never chooses such a stupid thing. But why do so many people follow them?

The reason is that people are not very confident. They don't know where to go, so they are just waiting for some messiah, somebody to tell them that this is the right path and to tell them with such certainty, with such obsessive certainty, that their fears are dissipated. So they say, "Yes, here is the leader. Now we will follow him. Here comes the right man—so confident!"

That confidence of the leader—which is because of stupidity—helps him to gather a great following, because people are lacking in courage, in confidence. They are stuck. They are afraid to move. They are almost paralyzed because of their hesitations. They need somebody who can become a torch and who is so confident that their own fear and lack of confidence does not trouble

> Confidence is not always a virtue. Intelligence is always a virtue. So insist on intelligence. Sometimes it will make you very hesitant, nervous. It has to be so . . . it is natural.

them. Now they can move with this man. They can say, "Yes, we are not confident, you are. Your confidence becomes a substitute for us."

So confidence is not always a virtue.

Intelligence is always a virtue. So insist on intelligence. Sometimes it will make you very hesitant, nervous. It has to be so . . . it is natural. Life is so complex and one is moving in the unknown continuously. How can one be confident? The very demand is absurd.

So make intelligence your goal and then hesitation, nervousness, everything, can be used in a creative way.

I can see that my mind is still childish. What can I do?

There are things which one has just to be aware of. The very awareness brings the transformation; it is not that after being aware you have to do something to make the change.

Seeing your mind as childish, you can also see that you are not the mind—otherwise, who is seeing the mind as childish? There is something beyond the mind—the watcher on the hills.

You are only looking at the mind. You have completely forgotten who is looking at it. Watch the mind, but don't forget the watcher— because your reality is centered in the watcher, not in the mind. And the watcher is always a fully grown-up, mature, centered consciousness. It needs no growth.

And once you become aware that the mind is only an instrument in the hands of your witnessing soul, then there is no problem; the mind can be used in the right way. Now the master is awake, and the servant can be ordered to do whatever is needed.

Ordinarily the master is asleep. We have forgotten the watcher, and the servant has become the master. And the servant is a servant—it is certainly not very intelligent.

You have to be reminded of a basic fact: Intelligence belongs to the watching consciousness; memory belongs to the mind.

Memory is one thing—memory is not intelligence. But the whole of humanity has been deceived for centuries and told indirectly that the memory is intelligence. Your schools, your colleges, your universities are not trying to find your intelligence; they are trying to find out who is capable of memorizing more.

And now we know perfectly well that memory is a mechanical thing. A computer can have memory, but a computer cannot have intelligence. And a computer can have a better memory than you have. Man's memory is not so reliable. It can forget, it can get mixed up, it can get blocked. Sometimes you say that "I remember it, it is just on the tip of my tongue." Strange, it is on the tip of your tongue, then why don't you speak?

But you say it is not coming, "It is on the tip of my tongue . . . I know that I know, and it is not very far—it is very close." But still some block, some very thin block—it may be just a curtain—is not allowing it to surface. And the more you try, the more tense you become, the smaller the possibility of remembering it. Finally, you forget all about it, you start doing something else—preparing a cup of tea or digging a hole in the garden—and suddenly it is there because you were relaxed, you had forgotten all about it, there was no tension. It surfaced.

A tense mind becomes narrow. A relaxed mind becomes wide—many more memories can pass through it. A tense mind becomes so narrow that only very few memories can pass through it.

> A tense mind becomes narrow. A relaxed mind becomes wide—many more memories can pass through it. A tense mind becomes so narrow that only very few memories can pass through it.

But for thousands of years a misunderstanding has continued, and it continues still, as if memory is intelligence. It is not.

In India—as in Arabia, China, Greece, Rome, in all old countries—all the old languages depend on memory, not on intelligence. You can become a great Sanskrit scholar without a bit of intelligence—no need for intelligence, just your memory has to be perfect. Just like a parrot . . . the parrot does not understand what he is saying, but he can say it absolutely correctly, with the right pronunciation. You can teach him whatever you want. All old languages depend on memory.

And the whole educational system of the world depends on memory. In the examinations, they don't ask the student something that will show his intelligence but something that will show his memory, how much he remembers from textbooks. This is one of the reasons for your retarded mind. You have used the memory as if it were your intelligence—a tremendously grave misunderstanding. Because you know and remember and you can quote scriptures, you start thinking that you are grown-up, you are mature, that you are knowledgeable, you are wise.

This is the problem, that you are feeling.

I am not a man of memory. And my effort here is to provoke a challenge in you so that you start moving toward your intelligence.

It is of no use how much you remember. What is significant is how much you have experienced yourself. And for experiencing the inner world, you need great intelligence—memory is of no help. Yes, if you want to be a scholar, a professor, a pundit, you can memorize scriptures and you can have a great pride that you know so much. And other people will also think that you know so much, and deep down your memory is nothing but ignorance.

In front of me, you cannot hide your ignorance. In every possible way, I try to bring your ignorance in front of you because the sooner you get hold of your ignorance, the sooner you can get rid of it. And to know is such a beautiful experience that the borrowed knowledge, in comparison, is just idiotic.

I have heard about the archbishop of Japan. He wanted to convert a Zen master to Christianity. Not knowing, not understanding anything of the inner world, he went to the master. He was received with great love and respect.

He opened his Bible and started reading the Sermon on the Mount. He wanted to impress upon the Zen master: We follow this man. What do you think about these words, about this man?

He had read only two sentences and the Zen master said, "That will do. You are following a good man, but he was following other good men. Neither you know nor does he know. Just go home."

The archbishop was very shocked. He said, "You should at least let me finish the whole thing."

The Zen master said, "No nonsense here. If you know something, you say it. Close the book! Because we are not believers in books. You are carrying the very truth in your being, and you are searching in dead books? Go home and look within. If you have found something inside, then come. If you think these lines that you have repeated to me are from Jesus Christ, you are wrong."

Jesus Christ was simply repeating the Old Testament. He was trying his whole life to convince people that "I am the last prophet of the Jews." He had never heard the word *Christian,* he had never heard the word *Christ.* He was born a Jew, he lived a Jew, he died a Jew. And his whole effort was to convince the Jews that "I am the awaited prophet, the savior that Moses has promised. I have come."

The Jews could have forgiven him . . . Jews are not bad people. And Jews are not violent people, either. Nobody who is as intelligent as the Jews are can be violent. Forty percent of Nobel prizes go to Jews; it is simply out of all proportion to their population. Almost half the Nobel prizes go to Jews, and the other half to the rest of the world. Such intelligent people would not have crucified Jesus if he had been saying something of his own experience. But he was saying things that were not his experience—all borrowed. Yet he was pretending they were his. Jews could not forgive that dishonesty.

Otherwise, Jesus was not creating any trouble for anybody. He was a little bit of a nuisance. Just like the Witnesses of Jehovah or the Hare Krishna people; they are a little bit of a nuisance. If they catch hold of you they will not listen to you at all and they will go on giving you all kinds of wisdom, advice—and you are not interested; you are going for some other work, you want to be left alone. But they are determined to save you. Whether you want to be saved or not does not matter—you have to be saved.

It happened that I was sitting near the Ganges in Allahabad, and it was just as the sun was setting. A man started shouting from the water, "Save me! Save me!" I am not interested in saving anybody. So I looked all around . . . if somebody is interested in saving him, let him have the first chance. But there was nobody, so finally I had to jump.

And with difficulty . . . he was a heavy man, fat. The fattest men in India you will find in Allahabad and Varanasi—the Brahmins, the Hindu priests, who do nothing except eat. Somehow I pulled him out. And he became angry. "Why did you pull me out?"

I said, "This is something! You were asking for help, you were shouting, 'Save me!'"

He said, "It was because I was becoming afraid of death. But in fact I was committing suicide."

I said, "I am sorry, I had no idea that you were committing suicide."

I pushed the man back! And he started shouting again, "Help!"

I said, "Now wait for somebody else to come. I will sit here and watch you commit suicide."

He said, "What kind of man are you? I am dying!"

I said, "Die! That is your business!"

But there are people who are bent upon saving you.

The Zen master said to the archbishop, "Jesus was repeating the old prophets. You are repeating Jesus. Repetition is not going to help anybody. You need your own experience—that is the only deliverance, the only liberation."

It is good that you are beginning to understand that your mind behaves like a child, immature. Remember also who is watching the childish, immature mind, and be with the watcher. Pull all your attachments away from the mind—because the mind is only a mechanism—and the mind will start functioning perfectly well. Once your watcher is alert, your intelligence starts growing for the first time.

Mind's work is memory, which the mind can do very well. But the mind has been burdened by the society with intelligence, which is not its work. It has crippled its memory. It has not made you more intelligent, it has simply made your memory erroneous, fallible.

Always remember: Your eyes are for seeing, don't try to listen with the eyes. Your ears are for listening, don't try to see with the ears. Otherwise, you will get into an insane state. While your eyes are perfectly all right, your ears are perfectly all right, you are trying to do something with a mechanism that is not meant to do it.

If your watcher is clear, then the body takes care of its own functions, the mind takes care of its own functions, the heart takes care of its own functions. Nobody interferes in each other's work.

And life becomes a harmony, an orchestra.

I sometimes feel muddle-headed, as if losing my memory.

Memory one day has to go completely. If it is disappearing, it is a good sign. To be clean of memory means to be clean of past, and to be clean of past is to be absolutely open and available to the future. Memory is not of the future, memory is of the past; it is always a graveyard. And the future belongs to life, to intelligence, to silence, to meditativeness. It does not belong to memory.

Once a man becomes enlightened he does not function out of memory, he functions spontaneously. And even on the path toward enlightenment, slowly spontaneity goes on replacing memory. Memory is the way of the unintelligent man. One who cannot respond to reality immediately needs a memory system so that he can remember old answers, old situations—what he has done before. But then his response is no longer a response, it becomes a reaction. And all reactions fall short of the situation that is ahead of you, because the situation is continuously changing and the answers in your memory don't change. They are just dead commodities, they remain the same.

That's why, as a person grows old, he finds himself getting out of touch with the new generation that is growing. The fault is not of the new generation, the fault is of the old man who has nothing but memory, and memory belongs to the past and the past is no longer there. The new generation is more responsive to the present—that creates the gap. The old generation always wants old answers, old scriptures, old saints; the older they are the more true this is.

Every religion tries to prove that their scriptures are the oldest. It is strange that they want to prove that. And they glory in their ancientness. In fact, the more ancient they are, the more useless they are, because they have lost touch with reality completely. The man of consciousness and wisdom, alive, actually responds to the situation. Otherwise all answers fall short and life becomes more and more a mess.

So there is no need to be worried about it, if you are losing your memory and you see that you don't feel any parallel upsurge of intelligence. You will not feel it. Intelligence is so subtle that you will not hear the sound of its footsteps. But slowly, slowly, it will transform your whole being and then suddenly, when the work is complete, you will awake from a deep sleep and you will see yourself as a new being, reborn.

If you start becoming more sharp, more intelligent, from where will you get the energy? The energy that is involved and invested in memories has to be withdrawn, and there is no harm in it. In the ordinary marketplace, perhaps, not to have a good memory can be dangerous. But if you look at the geniuses of the world, you will be surprised that one of the most common points among all those geniuses is their lapse of memory.

Edison is going for a lecture tour to a few universities. He is saying good-bye to his wife and the maidservant is also standing there. He kisses the maidservant, thinking that she is his wife, and waves to his wife, thinking that she is the maidservant. The driver of the car who was taking him cannot believe what is happening.

He said, "Sir, you have forgotten, you have got mixed up. The woman whom you are waving to is your wife and the other woman is your servant."

He said, "My God. There is no harm, I can get out of the car and put things right." He kissed his wife, waved to the maidservant, and he said, "It often happens that I forget very essential things."

Once, George Bernard Shaw was traveling in a train. The ticket checker came and Bernard Shaw looked all over, he almost felt like he was having a nervous breakdown because the ticket could not be found. The ticket checker said, "Don't be worried, sir. I know you, the whole world knows you. The ticket must be somewhere in your luggage and I will be coming in the next round, you can show me then—and even if you don't show me there is no need to worry." He was not ready to listen to what Bernard Shaw said to him: "You shut up. You don't understand my problem. Who cares about you? The problem is if I don't find my ticket, then I don't know where I am going. It is written on the ticket. So are you going to decide for me? I am in such trouble, the ticket has to be found."

The ticket checker must have been taken aback—this was a strange situation. Shaw was not worried about being caught without a ticket, his worry was far deeper. Now the question was, where was he going? And because he could not find the ticket he had to go back home on the next train. He could not bring to his memory the place he was going to.

But for the most part, each moment intelligence is needed, not memory. My own understanding is that if we want to make humanity more conscious, more alert, more enlightened, then the emphasis has to be taken away from memory; the emphasis has to be put on intelligence.

But for universities, for professors, for pedagogues, emphasis on memory is simpler. You just ask five questions and if the person can memorize the books, he can answer them.

My own professor was very much worried—because he loved me so much—because I never bothered about the prescribed books. And he was so concerned: "Unless you answer exactly what is written in the books, it will be a great shock to all of us. You have the capacity to top the whole university, but the way you are behaving you cannot even pass."

I said, "Don't be worried." But he was so concerned that he used to come early in the morning to pick me up from the hostel and take me to the examination hall. He was not certain whether I would go or not, whether I would remember to go or not. And he would stand there until I had gone in and he would tell every examiner, "Keep an eye on this student, don't let him get out of the hall before the three hours are over, because he may answer within one hour and be gone. Force him, whether he has answered or not, to be here for three hours."

I said, "This is strange . . ." But the examiners listened to him because he was also the dean of the Faculty of Arts.

All my professors, my vice chancellors, everybody was so surprised when I topped the university and got the gold medal. Nobody was expecting that. But a coincidence—one of the most famous professors of Allahabad University, Professor Ranade . . . It was well known that in his life he had given only two persons first class. Those two were the bare minimum. Otherwise it was very difficult even to get passing marks from him. And he was thought to be not only a professor but a sage. He had written great books with great insight; there was no doubt about his intellectual acumen. Just by coincidence my papers reached his hands. And he wrote a note, which the vice chancellor showed to me because Professor Ranade had written, "This note should be shown to the student." He said, "You are the only person in my life who has fulfilled my desire. I always hated memorized answers; your answers are so fresh and so short, to the point. You are not a man of memory. I wanted to give you a hundred percent, but that may look a little suspicious—perhaps I am favoring you—that's why I am giving you ninety-nine percent. But if you happen to come to Allahabad any time, I would love to meet you. In my whole lifelong career as a professor, I have been waiting for you. I wanted these kinds of answers. I wanted this courage—rather than answering the question, you questioned the question and you demolished the question completely. You have not answered it because there is nothing to answer; the question is absurd. And when you answer a question, you answer to the point. I don't want to read long answers, which are all repetitive. Everybody else is writing them, nobody is using his intelligence."

He was aware of the fact that memory is only mechanical; intelligence is your real treasure. And now it has become an absolute fact. In the future, memory will not be used at all, because you can carry a small computer in a pocket with all the answers for all the questions that can be asked. Even absurd questions . . . for example, on what day Socrates was married. Or, who was the first man to use the bow and arrow. Everything can be ready-made. You can get any answer from the computer.

And computers can be so small that you can keep them in your pocket. They can be so small that you can make just a wristwatch out of them. On the surface it will look like a wristwatch, but deep down it is carrying all the answers that you need. Just ask the question and the answer is there.

You don't have to be worried about your memory. What is essential is intelligence. And the whole energy should move toward intelligence. It will make you feel very light. And as far as memory is concerned, just use a notebook. Anything essential, fundamental, just note it down. Then there is no leakage. Leakage as such never happens.

Paddy, Sean, and Mick were out hunting one day when they came upon some tracks. After looking at them closely, Paddy said, "Those are bear tracks."

"No, no," said Sean, "those are deer tracks."

"Hey, Mick," they both asked, "what do you think they are?"

But before he could answer, all three were hit by a train.

Intelligence is going to be the savior, not memory.

How can lovers behave more intelligently?

When you have moved in deep relationship with somebody, a great need arises to be alone. You start feeling spent, exhausted, tired—joyously tired, happily tired, but each excitement is exhausting. It was tremendously beautiful to relate, but now you would like to move into aloneness, so that you can again gather yourself together, so that again you can become overflowing, so that again you become rooted in your own being.

In love you moved into the other's being, you lost contact with yourself. You became drowned, drunk. Now you will need to find yourself again. But when you are alone, you are again creating a need for love. Soon you will be so full that you would like to share, you will be so overflowing that you would like somebody to pour yourself into, to whom to give of yourself. Love arises out of aloneness.

Aloneness makes you overfull. Love receives your gifts. Love empties you so that you can become full again. Whenever you are emptied by love, aloneness is there to nourish you, to integrate you. And this is a rhythm.

Make your woman or your man also alert to the rhythm. People should be taught that nobody can love twenty-four hours a day; rest periods are needed. And nobody can love on order. Love is a spontaneous phenomenon: Whenever it happens, it happens, and whenever it doesn't happen it doesn't happen. Nothing can be done about it. If you DO anything, you will create a pseudo phenomenon, an acting.

Real lovers, intelligent lovers, will make each other alert to the phenomenon: "When I want to be alone that does not mean that I am rejecting you. In fact, it is because of your love that you have made it possible for me to be alone." And if your woman wants to be left alone for one night, for a few days, you will not feel hurt. You will not say that you have been rejected, that your love has not been received and welcomed. You will respect her decision to be alone for a few days. In fact, you will be happy! Your love was so much that she is feeling empty; now she needs rest to become full again.

This is intelligence.

Ordinarily, you think you are rejected. You go to your woman, and if she is not willing to be with you, or not very loving to you, you feel great rejection. Your ego is hurt. This ego is not a very intelligent thing. All egos are idiotic. Intelligence knows no ego; intelligence simply sees the phenomenon, tries to understand why the woman does not want to be with you. Not that she is rejecting you—you know she has loved you so much, she loves you so much—but this is a moment she wants to be alone. And if you love her, you will leave her alone; you will not torture her, you will not force her to make love to you.

And if the man wants to be alone, the woman will not think, "He is no longer interested in me—maybe he has become interested in some other woman." An intelligent woman will leave the man alone, so he can again gather together his being, so that again he has energy to share. And this rhythm is like day and night, summer and winter; it goes on changing.

And if two persons are really respectful—and love is always respectful, it reveres the other; it is a very worshipful, prayerful state—then slowly you will understand each other more and more. And you will become aware of the other's rhythm and your rhythm. And soon you will find that out of love, out of respect, your rhythms are coming closer and closer: When you feel loving, she feels loving. This settles. This settles on its own. It is a synchronicity.

Have you watched ever? If you come across two real lovers, you will see many things similar in them. Real lovers become as if they are brothers and sisters. You will be surprised—even brothers and sisters are not so

> Love gives freedom and love helps the other to be himself or herself. Love is a very paradoxical phenomenon. In one way it makes you one soul in two bodies, in another way it gives you individuality, uniqueness.

alike. Their expressions, their ways of walking, their ways of talking, their gestures—two lovers become alike, and yet so different. This naturally starts happening. Just being together, slowly they become attuned to each other. Real lovers need not say anything to the other—the other immediately understands, intuitively understands.

If the woman is sad, she may not say it is so, but the man understands and leaves her alone. If the man is sad, the woman understands and leaves him alone—finds some excuse to leave him alone. Stupid people do just the opposite: They never leave each other alone—they are constantly with each other, tiring and boring each other; never leaving any space for the other to be.

Love gives freedom and love helps the other to be himself or herself. Love is a very paradoxical phenomenon. In one way it makes you one soul in two bodies; in another way it gives you individuality, uniqueness. It helps you to drop your small selves, but it also helps you to attain to the supreme self. Then there is no problem: Love and meditation are two wings, and they balance each other. And between the two you grow.

Sometimes I have doubts about my intelligence.

Don't start thinking that if you are not intelligent, then what? Everybody is born intelligent. Intelligence is an intrinsic quality—just as everybody is born breathing, everybody is born intelligent.

The idea that a few people are intelligent and a few are not is utterly wrong—and has been dehumanizing many, many people. It is very insulting, degrading. All are born intelligent, although their intelligences may differ in their expressions. One is intelligent in music, another is intelligent in mathematics, but if you make mathematics the criterion then the musician looks unintelligent. If you put them both into one examination where mathematics is the criterion, the musician fails. Change the criterion, let music be the criterion, and put them both into the examination where music will decide, then the mathematician looks stupid.

We have chosen certain criteria; that's why many people have been condemned as stupid—they are not. I have never come across a single person who is stupid—it does not happen—but his intelligence may be a different kind of intelligence. Poetry needs a different kind of intelligence than being in business. A poet cannot be a businessman, and the businessman will find it very difficult to be a poet. One kind of intelligence is needed in being a politician, another kind of intelligence is needed in being a painter. And there are millions of possibilities.

Remember: Everyone is born intelligent, so that is not excluding anybody. You just have to find your intelligence—where it is. And once you have found your intelligence you will be clear.

> I have never come across a single person who is stupid—it does not happen—but his intelligence may be a different kind of intelligence.

People are living with unclarity because they are living with wrong ideas about themselves. Somebody has told you—a teacher, a professor, an employer—that you are not intelligent. But their criterion is only a chosen criterion; their criterion is not applicable to all. The universities are not yet universal. They don't allow every kind of intelligence, they don't accept all manifestations of intelligence.

Once you have accepted your intelligence and you start respecting it, you will become clear; there will be no problem.

The poet feels stupid because he cannot be a good businessman. Now this creates confusion. He becomes inferior in his own eyes, disrespectful, condemning. He tries to succeed in business but he cannot. This creates great smoke around him. If he simply understands that he is a poet and he is not meant to be a businessman, and to succeed as a businessman will be a suicide to him, he has to succeed as a poet . . . That is his intelligence, and his intelligence has to flower in his own way. He has not to imitate anybody else. Maybe the society will not pay for it, because poetry is not needed as much as bombs are needed. Love is not needed as much as hatred is needed.

That's why in the films, on the radio, on the television, murder is allowed; it is not called obscene. But lovemaking is called obscene. This society lives through hate not through love. If somebody is murdering, it is perfectly okay. If somebody puts a dagger into your heart and the blood rushes like a fountain, it is perfectly okay. But if somebody hugs you, kisses you, loves you, the society is afraid.

This is strange, that love is obscene and murder is not, that lovers are condemned and soldiers rewarded, that war is right and love is wrong.

If you accept your intelligence, if you accept yourself, you will become clear, absolutely clear; all clouds will disappear.

How can I support my own growth of intelligence?

First become more and more alert in small things. Walking along the road, become more alert, try to be more alert. For such a simple process as walking along the road you need not have any alertness. You can remain stupid and walk well. That's what everyone is doing. The stupidity does not hinder you at all. Start from small things. Taking your bath, be alert; standing under the shower, become very alert. That cold water falling on you, the body enjoying it . . . become alert, become conscious of what is happening, be relaxed yet conscious.

And this moment of consciousness has to be brought in again and again, in a thousand and one ways: eating, talking, meeting a friend, listening to me, meditating, making love. In all situations try to become more and more alert. It is hard, it is certainly difficult, but it is not impossible. Slowly, slowly, the dust will disappear and your mirrorlike consciousness will reveal itself; you will become more intelligent.

Then live intelligently. You live in such a confused way, in such a stupid way, that if you saw somebody else living that way you would immediately say that he is stupid. But you are doing the same, although somehow one manages not to look at one's own life.

A man came to me and he said, "What to do, Osho? I have fallen in love with two women." Now one is enough, one will do enough harm, but he has fallen in love with two women. So both are struggling and he is crushed. And he says, "I am in misery. Both are fighting over me." And naturally from both sides he is being hit! And if I say to him, "Choose one," he says that it is difficult. This means that one person is riding on two horses. He says it is difficult to choose one. Then let it be, have it your own way. You will destroy your life. Choosing two women or two men as your love objects is bound to split you. You will start falling apart.

This is stupid. It is so simple to look into the phenomenon. Maybe sometimes it is difficult—it *is* difficult—but then too one has to choose. You cannot go in all the directions simultaneously.

If you look into your life you will find how unintelligently you have been behaving. You read a book and you accumulate knowledge and you start thinking that you know. You have learned the word *God* and you think you have known God. You are ready to argue—not only argue, you are ready to kill and be killed. How many Mohammedans, how many Hindus, how many Christians, have been killed for something they have read only in a book! Tremendously stupid people. One is fighting for the Koran, another is fighting for the Gita, another is fighting for the Bible—for books you are fighting and killing living people and sacrificing your tremendously valuable life! What are you doing?

But man has behaved in stupid ways. Just because everybody else is behaving in the same way does not make it intelligent. If all are fools it does not make you intelligent because you are following them.

I have heard.

A flock of birds was flying into the sky and one bird asked another, "Why do we always follow this stupid leader?"

And the other said, "I don't know. I have heard that only he has the map."

179

The map! Nobody has the map. But you go on following the pope, the Shankaracharya, the pundit, the politician, and you think they have the map, you think they know. Just look into their lives—what do they know? They may even be far more stupid than you are. Just look at the unintelligent way they are living. Watch their life. Are they happy? Is there a dance in their life? Is there fragrance in their life? Just looking at them do you feel a silence showering on you? Nothing of the sort. Just because they have a book and they have read it and studied it for years, it does not make any sense to follow them.

Become a person of knowing, not a person of knowledge. Then you live intelligently.

To me intelligence is the basic morality, the basic virtue. If you are intelligent you will not harm anybody because that is foolish. If you are intelligent you will not harm yourself because that is foolish. Life is so precious, it is not to be wasted; it has to be lived in deep celebration, in deep gratitude.

And one has to be very careful and watchful because a moment gone is gone forever. It will never return. So if you waste it in stupidity you are wasting a great opportunity. Live each moment so totally, so fully aware, that you never repent later on that you didn't live, that you could have lived more, that you could have enjoyed more. That's what intelligence is: to live life so totally that there is no repentance, ever. One is always contented. One knows that one has lived to one's utmost.

> Live each moment so totally, so fully aware, that you never repent later on that you didn't live, that you could have lived more, that you could have enjoyed more. That's what intelligence is: to live life so totally that there is no repentance, never.

Afterword

REDISCOVERING INTELLIGENCE
THROUGH MEDITATION

There is a switch in the mind. The name of the switch is watchfulness, awareness, witnessing. If you start witnessing the mind it begins to stop. The more that witnessing grows, the more and more do you become aware of a secret key, that the mind can be stopped easily. And that moment is of great liberation, when you can turn the mind off for hours. And when it comes back, when you recall it, it comes back rejuvenated, fresh.

Hence meditators are bound to be more intelligent than other people. If they are not then their meditation is false, then they don't know what meditation is; they are doing something else in the name of meditation. A meditative person is bound to be more sensitive, more intelligent, more creative, more loving, more compassionate. These qualities grow of their own accord. And the whole secret is in one thing: Learn to stop the mind. The moment you know how to stop the mind you become the master, and then mind is a beautiful mechanism. You use it when you want to use it, when it is needed, and you put it off when it is not needed.

Afterword

* ★ *

What is meditation? Is it a technique that can be practiced? Is it an effort that you have to do? Is it something which the mind can achieve? It is not.

All that the mind can do cannot be meditation—it is something beyond the mind, the mind is absolutely helpless there. The mind cannot penetrate meditation; where mind ends, meditation begins. This has to be remembered, because in our life, whatsoever we do, we do through the mind; whatsoever we achieve, we achieve through the mind. And then, when we turn inward, we again start thinking in terms of techniques, methods, doings, because the whole of life's experience shows us that everything can be done by the mind. Yes. Except meditation, everything can be done by the mind; everything is done by the mind except meditation. Because meditation is not an achievement—it is already the case, it is your nature. It has not to be achieved; it has only to be recognized, it has only to be remembered. It is there waiting for you—just a turning in, and it is available. You have been carrying it always and always.

Meditation is your intrinsic nature—it is you, it is your being, it has nothing to do with your doings. You cannot have it, you cannot not have it, it cannot be possessed. It is not a thing. It is you. It is your being.

> Meditation is not an achievement—it is already the case, it is your nature. It has not to be achieved, it has only to be recognized, it has only to be remembered. It is there waiting for you—just a turning in, and it is available. You have been carrying it always.

Once you understand what meditation is things become very clear. Otherwise, you can go on groping in the dark.

Meditation is a state of clarity, not a state of mind. Mind is confusion. Mind is never clear. It cannot be. Thoughts create clouds around you—they are subtle clouds. A mist is created by them, and the clarity is lost. When thoughts disappear, when there are no more clouds around you, when you are in your simple beingness, clarity happens. Then you can see far away; then you can see to the very end of existence; then your gaze becomes penetrating—to the very core of being.

Meditation is clarity, absolute clarity, of vision. You cannot think about it. You have to drop thinking. When I say, "You have to drop thinking," don't conclude in a hurry, because I have to use language. So I say, "Drop thinking," but if *you* start *dropping* you will miss, because again you will reduce it to a doing.

"Drop thinking" simply means: Don't do anything. Sit. Let thoughts settle themselves. Let mind drop of its own accord. You just sit gazing at the wall, in a silent corner, not doing anything at all. Relaxed. Loose. With no effort. Not going anywhere. As if you are falling asleep awake— you are awake and you are relaxing but the whole body is falling into sleep. You remain alert inside but the whole body moves into deep relaxation.

Thoughts settle of their own accord, you need not jump among them, you need not try to put them right. It is as if a stream has become muddy . . . what do you do? Do you jump in it and start helping the stream to become clear? You will make it more muddy. You simply sit on the bank. You wait. There is nothing to be done. Because whatsoever you do will make the stream more muddy. If somebody has passed through a stream and the dead leaves have surfaced and the mud has arisen, just patience is needed. You simply sit on the bank. Watch, indifferently. And as the stream goes on flowing, the dead leaves will be taken away, and the mud will start settling because it cannot hang forever.

After a while, suddenly you will become aware—the stream is crystal clear again.

Whenever a desire passes through your mind the stream becomes muddy. So just sit. Don't try to do anything. In Japan this "just sitting" is called *Zazen;* just sitting and doing nothing. And one day, meditation happens. Not that you bring it to you; it comes to you. And when it comes, you immediately recognize it; it has been always there but you were not looking in the right direction. The treasure has been with you but you were occupied somewhere else: in thoughts, in desires, in a thousand and one things. You were not interested in the only one thing . . . and that was your own being.

Remember, meditation will bring you more and more intelligence, infinite intelligence, a radiant intelligence. Meditation will make you more alive and sensitive; your life will become richer.

You can go into meditation just by sitting, but then be just sitting; do not do anything else. If you can be just sitting, it becomes meditation. Be completely in the sitting; nonmovement should be your only movement. In fact, the word *Zen* comes from the word *Zazen,* which means, just sitting, doing nothing. If you can just sit, doing nothing with your body and nothing with your mind, it becomes meditation; but it is difficult.

You can sit very easily when you are doing something else, but the moment you are just sitting and doing nothing, it becomes a problem. Every fiber of the body begins to move inside; every vein, every muscle, begins to move. You will begin to feel a subtle trembling; you will be aware of many points in the body of which you have never been aware before. And the more you try to just sit, the more movement you will feel inside you. So sitting can be used only if you have done other things first.

You can just walk, that is easier. You can just dance, that is even easier. And after you have been doing other things that are easier, then you can sit. Sitting in a buddha posture is the last thing to do, really; it should never be done in the beginning. Only after you have begun to feel identified totally with movement can you begin to feel totally identified with nonmovement.

So I never tell people to begin with just sitting. Begin from where beginning is easy, otherwise you will begin to feel many things unnecessarily—things that are not there.

If you begin with sitting, you will feel much disturbance inside. The more you try to just sit, the more disturbance will be felt; you will become aware only of your insane mind and nothing else. It will create depression, you will feel frustrated. You will not feel blissful; rather, you will begin to feel that you are insane. And sometimes you may really go insane.

If you make a sincere effort to "just sit," you may really go insane. Only because people do not really try sincerely does insanity not happen more often. With a sitting posture you begin to know so much madness inside you that if you are sincere and continue it, you may really go insane. It has happened before, so many times; so I never suggest anything that can create frustration, depression, sadness—anything that will allow you to be too aware of your insanity. You may not be ready to be aware of all the insanity that is inside you; you must be allowed to get to know certain things gradually. Knowledge is not always good; it must unfold itself slowly as your capacity to absorb it grows.

I begin with your insanity, not with a sitting posture; I allow your insanity. If you dance madly, the opposite happens within you. With a mad dance, you begin to be aware of a silent point within you; with sitting silently, you begin to be aware of madness. The opposite is always the point of awareness. With your dancing madly, chaotically, with crying, with chaotic breathing, I allow your madness. Then you begin to be aware of a subtle point, a deep point inside you which is silent and still, in contrast to the madness on the periphery. You will feel very blissful; at your center there is an inner silence. But if you are just sitting, then the inner one is the mad one; you are silent on the outside, but inside you are mad.

If you begin with something active—something positive, alive, moving—it will be better; then you will begin to feel an inner stillness growing. The more it grows, the more it will be possible for you to use a sitting posture or a lying posture—the more silent meditation will be possible. But by then things will be different, totally different.

A meditation technique that begins with movement, action, helps you in other ways, also. It becomes a catharsis. When you are just sitting, you are frustrated; your mind wants to move and you are just sitting. Every muscle turns, every nerve turns. You are trying to force something upon yourself that is not natural for you; then you have divided yourself into the one who is forcing and the one who is being forced. And really, the part that is being forced and suppressed is the more authentic part; it is a more major part of your mind than the part that is suppressing, and the major part is bound to win.

That which you are suppressing is really to be thrown, not suppressed. It has become an accumulation within you because you have been constantly suppressing it. The whole upbringing, the civilization, the education, is suppressive. You have been suppressing much that could have been thrown very easily with a different education, with a more conscious education, with a more aware parenthood. With a better awareness of the inner mechanism of the mind, the culture could have allowed you to throw many things.

For example, when a child is angry we tell him, "Do not be angry." He begins to suppress anger. By and by, what was a momentary happening becomes permanent. Now he will not act angry, but he will remain angry. We have accumulated so much anger from what were just momentary things; no one can be angry continuously unless anger has been suppressed. Anger is a momentary thing that comes and goes: If it is expressed, then you are no longer angry. So with me, I would allow the child to be angry more authentically. Be angry, but be deep in it; do not suppress it.

Of course, there will be problems. If we say, "Be angry," then you are going to be angry at someone. But a child can be molded; he can be given a pillow and told, "Be angry with the pillow. Be violent with the pillow." From the very beginning, a child can be brought up in a way in which the anger is just deviated. Some object can be given to him: He can go on throwing the object until his anger goes. Within minutes, within seconds, he will have dissipated his anger and there will be no accumulation of it.

You have accumulated anger, sex, violence, greed, everything! Now this accumulation is a madness within you. It is there, inside you. If you begin with any suppressive meditation—for example, with just sitting—you are suppressing all of this, you are not allowing it to be released. So I begin with a catharsis. First, let the suppressions be thrown into the air; and when you can throw your anger into the air, you have become mature.

If I cannot be loving alone, if I can be loving only with someone I love, then, really, I am not mature yet. Then I am depending on someone even to be loving; someone must be there, then I can be loving. Then that loving can only be a very superficial thing; it is not my nature. If I am alone in the room I am not loving at all, so the loving quality has not gone deep; it has not become a part of my being.

You become more and more mature when you are less and less dependent. If you can be angry alone, you are more mature. You do not need any object to be angry. So I make a catharsis in the beginning a must. You must throw everything into the sky, into the open space, without being conscious of any object.

Be angry without the person with whom you would like to be angry. Weep without finding any cause; laugh, just laugh, without anything to laugh at. Then you can just throw the whole accumulated thing—you can just throw it. And once you know the way, you are unburdened of the whole past.

Within moments you can be unburdened of the whole life—of lives even. If you are ready to throw everything, if you can allow your madness to come out, within moments there is a deep cleansing. Now you are cleansed: fresh, innocent—you are a child again. Now, in your innocence, sitting meditation can be done—just sitting, or just lying, or anything—because now there is no mad one inside to disturb the sitting.

Cleansing must be the first thing—a catharsis—otherwise, with breathing exercises, with just sitting, with practicing yoga asanas, postures, you are just suppressing something.

When silence comes to you, when it descends on you, it is not a false thing. You have not been cultivating it; it comes to you; it happens to you. You begin to feel it growing inside you just like a mother begins to feel a child growing. A deep silence is growing inside you; you become pregnant with it. Only then is there transformation; otherwise it is just self-deception. And one can deceive oneself for lives and lives—the capacity to do so is infinite.

Intelligence can be rediscovered. The only method to rediscover it is meditation. Meditation only does one thing: It destroys all the barriers that the society has created to prevent you from being intelligent. It simply removes the blocks. Its function is negative: It removes the rocks that are preventing your waters from flowing, your springs from becoming alive. Everybody is carrying the great potential, but society has put great rocks to prevent it. It has created China Walls around you; it has imprisoned you.

If you are a Christian you are imprisoned by the Christian priests. If you are a Hindu you are imprisoned by Hindu priests. Your prisons are different; maybe their architecture is different, the rooms are made differently, with different material. And maybe a few prisons are more comfortable than others, more sophisticated than others. Of course the American prison is better than the Indian prison, far better, more comfortable: the radio is available, the TV is available to the prisoner. The Indian prison is bound to be Indian. Indians are living in such an uncomfortable way, how can they provide television and radio and comfort to the prisoners? Impossible. They are there to be punished; they cannot be allowed to enjoy.

Christianity may be a little better prison than Mohammedanism, but a prison is a prison. And in fact a better prison is far more dangerous because you may start clinging to it, you may not like to get out of it; you may start loving it as if it is your home. But these are all prisons.

And sometimes people get fed up with one prison and they change their prisons. The Hindu becomes the Christian, the Christian becomes the Hindu. Now there are many foolish Christians who have become Hare Krishna people—the same stupidity but masquerading in a new form. There are many Hindus who have become Christians, but the same superstitiousness persists; there is no difference at all. I have seen those Hindus who have become Christians—no change. I have seen those Christians who have become Hindus—no change. They have just changed the prison.

To come out of all prisons is intelligence—and never to get into another again. Intelligence can be discovered through meditation because all those prisons exist in your mind. They cannot reach your being, fortunately. They cannot pollute your being, they can only pollute your mind—they can only cover your mind. If you can get out of the mind you will get out of Christianity, Hinduism, Jainism, Buddhism, and all kinds of rubbish will be just finished. You can come to a full stop.

And when you are out of the mind, watching it, being aware of it, just being a witness, you are intelligent. Your intelligence is discovered. You have undone what the society has done to you; you have destroyed the mischief; you have destroyed the conspiracy of the priests and the politicians. You have come out of it, you are free. In fact, you are for the first time a real human being, an authentic human being. Now the whole sky is yours.

About the Author

Osho's teachings defy categorization, covering everything from the individual quest for meaning to the most urgent social and political issues facing society today. His books are not written but are transcribed from audio and video recordings of extemporaneous talks given to international audiences over a period of thirty-five years. Osho has been described by the *Sunday Times* in London as one of the "1,000 Makers of the 20th Century" and by American author Tom Robbins as "the most dangerous man since Jesus Christ."

About his own work Osho has said that he is helping to create the conditions for the birth of a new kind of human being. He has often characterized this new human being as "Zorba the Buddha"—capable of enjoying both the earthy pleasures of a Zorba the Greek and the silent serenity of a Gautam Buddha. Running like a thread through all aspects of Osho's work is a vision that encompasses both the timeless wisdom of the East and the highest potential of Western science and technology.

Osho is also known for his revolutionary contribution to the science of inner transformation, with an approach to meditation that acknowledges the accelerated pace of contemporary life. His unique "Active Meditations" are designed to first release the accumulated stresses of body and mind, so that it is easier to experience the thought-free and relaxed state of meditation.

Osho® Meditation Resort

The Osho Meditation Resort is a place where people can have a direct personal experience of a new way of living with more alertness, relaxation, and fun. Located about one hundred miles southeast of Mumbai in Pune, India, the resort offers a variety of programs to thousands of people who visit each year from more than a hundred countries around the world.

Originally developed as a summer retreat for maharajas and wealthy British colonialists, Pune is now a thriving modern city that is home to a number of universities and high-tech industries. The meditation resort spreads over forty acres in a tree-lined suburb known as Koregaon Park. The resort campus provides accommodation for a limited number of guests, and there is a plentiful variety of nearby hotels and private apartments available for stays of a few days up to several months.

Resort programs are all based on the Osho vision of a qualitatively new kind of human being who is able both to participate creatively in everyday life and to relax into silence and meditation. Most programs take place in modern, air-conditioned facilities and include a variety of individual sessions, courses, and workshops covering everything from creative arts to holistic health treatments, personal transformation and therapy, esoteric sciences, the "Zen" approach to sports and recreation, relationship issues, and significant life transitions for men and women. Individual sessions and group workshops are offered throughout the year, alongside a full daily schedule of meditations.

Outdoor cafes and restaurants within the resort grounds serve both traditional Indian fare and a choice of international dishes, all made with organically grown vegetables from the commune's own farm. The campus has its own private supply of safe, filtered water.

For more information about Osho and his work, see:

www.osho.com

This is a comprehensive Web site in several languages, featuring an online tour of the meditation resort, a calendar of its course offerings, a catalog of books and tapes, a list of Osho information centers worldwide, and selections from Osho's talks.

Or contact:

Osho International
New York
e-mail: oshointernational@oshointernational.com

OSHO®

LOOK WITHIN...

TAO: THE PATHLESS PATH

Contemporary interpretations of selected parables from the *Lieh Tzu* reveal how the timeless wisdom of this 2500-year-old Taoist classic contains priceless insight for living today.

ISBN: 1-58063-225-4 Paperback $11.95/$17.95 Can.

YOGA: THE SCIENCE OF THE SOUL

Modern yoga emphasizes physical postures and exercises to increase flexibility and aid in relaxation. But yoga has its roots in the understanding of human consciousness and its potential. Explore this potential with Osho's unique insights into yoga and its relationship to the modern mind.

ISBN: 0-312-30614-8 Paperback $12.95/$18.95 Can.

ZEN: THE PATH OF PARADOX

"Zen is not a philosophy, it is poetry. It does not propose, it simply persuades. It does not argue, it simply sings its own song. It is aesthetic to the very core." In *Zen*, Osho unfolds the paradox of modern life through delightful Zen anecdotes and riddles.

ISBN: 0-312-32049-3 Paperback $11.95/$17.95 Can.

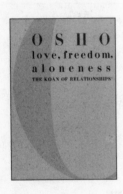